Bermudian Cookery

Published by
the
Bermuda Junior Service League

Cover and Photographs: Stephen Bainbridge
Architectural Sketches: Stephen West
Culinary Sketches: Diana Amos
Layout and Design: Peter Marsh

Printed in Bermuda by the Island Press Ltd.

Printed November 1974 — 5,000
2nd Edition March 1975 — 10,000

Cookery Book Committee

Bermudian Cookery
may be obtained by writing
The Bermuda Junior Service League,
Post Office Box 1226,
Hamilton 5, BERMUDA

Price per copy: U.S. $4.50 surface mail, $5.00 air mail
U.K. £2 surface mail, £2.20 air mail
for your convenience, an order blank is enclosed on page 191

All proceeds from the sale of this book will be returned to the community
through the various projects of the Bermuda Junior Service League.

Have you ever made a "Navarin" or a "trifle" or "weisse maeuse" or "conch fritters" or "anticuchos"? You will find receipts for these and many more intriguing dishes in our cookery book. As Bermuda is a melting pot of all nations so the Bermuda Junior Service League is a conglomeration of nationalities. In this cookery book we have tried to present a mixture of old Bermudian receipts, restaurant specialities and other favourite receipts ... depending upon where we or our husbands come from ... be it Bermuda, England, Canada, France, Germany, Chile or the United States.

Of course, you will find differences in spelling and we have left them purposely as they reflect our diverse languages. One spelling that should be explained is that of Sir George Somers' flagship the *Sea 'Venture*. There is an apostrophe before the "V" because the ship was originally called the *Sea Adventure*, but with usage the "Ad" was dropped. And also, words have different meanings: *maize* in England is *corn* in America. It was originally called *Indian corn* in Bermuda and now just *corn*.

This is not a basic cook book so we assume that everyone knows that ovens must be preheated even though this may not be specified in each receipt. Ingredients are often given in both weights and measures.

Intensive research was done on the section "Bermuda's Bounty" and we have many friends to thank for their help: Mrs Charles Burland, Mrs Morris Cooper, the late Mrs Vaughan Pugh, Mrs Rendell Arton, Mr and Mrs William E.S. Zuill, Mr Charles Pearman-Wilson, Mrs Elise White, Mrs Dixon Spurling, Mrs Myrtle Hollis, Mrs Bill Williams, Mrs Gayous Powell, Mrs E.C. Davis, Mrs Rodney Ferguson, the late Miss May Frith, Miss Sally Lewis, Mrs Alfred Darrell, Miss Esther Dickinson, Mrs Elton Wayland, Mr Graeme Outerbridge and Mrs Charles E. Malone.

The cover picture was taken in the kitchen of the St. George's Historical Museum. We are very grateful to Mrs Horace Frith, curator of the museum, for her help.

This book would not have been possible without the aid of Mr Don French, Mr Stephen Bainbridge and Mr Colin Hind of Aardvark Advertising. And what would we have done without Mrs Terry Tucker. She not only searched out obscure culinary lore in the Bermuda Research Library and read the preliminary drafts of the historical section, but was always ready with an encouraging word and a witty ancedote.

Many, many thanks to everyone, and a special thank you to the many husbands and children who were understanding when the typewriters pounded late and meal hours were rather erratic. May you all now sit down to out-of-the-ordinary repasts.

Margaret de Marcy

Contents

Bermuda's Bounty
A History of Bermudian Cookery from 1609 to the Present

Chefs' Choices
Receipts from Bermudian Restaurants

Rock-Happy Receipts
Menus from Members of the Bermuda Junior Service League

Bermuda's Bounty
A History of Bermudian Cookery
from 1609 to
the Present

Culinary Drawings
Appearing on the Following Pages

❄ ❄ ❄ ❄ ❄ ❄ ❄ ❄ ❄

Photograph from interior of the replica of the ship "Deliverance" built by the Bermuda Junior Service League in 1971 and open daily in St. Georges.

❄ ❄ ❄ ❄ ❄ ❄ ❄ ❄ ❄

"These Islands of the *Bermudos* have euer beene accounted as an in-chaunted pile of rockes, and a desert inhabitation for Diuils; but all the Fairies of the rockes were but flocks of birds, and all the Diuils that haunted the woods, were but heards of swine".

A True Declaration of the Estate of the Colonie in Virginie [published in London, 1610]

And how happy Admiral Sir George Somers and the 150 passengers on the *Sea 'Venture* must have been to see these islands called the Bermudas on the morning of Friday, July 28th, 1609. After floundering in a storm and losing the other ships in their fleet taking supplies from England to Jamestown they wedged their ship between two rocks. All the passengers and unspoiled goods were taken ashore. We have accurate accounts of these first months in Bermuda written by two passengers of the *Sea 'Venture*: William Strachey, the secretary of Sir Thomas Gates who was on his way to Virginia to serve as deputy governor, and Silvester Jourdain, a passenger. It is probable that Shakspere had read both these works before writing "The Tempest".

Once the castaways were on land Sir George Somers set about finding food and "in half an hour he took so many great fishes with hooks as did suffice the whole company one day. And fish is there so abundant that if a man step into the water they will come round about him; so that men were fain to get out for fear of biting. These fishes are very fat and sweet and of that proportion and bigness that three of them will conveniently lade two men: those we called rockfish".

The rockfish continues to be one of the most popular fish in Bermuda and is nearly always found on local restaurant menus. Here is an unusual old receipt from St. David's Island.

ROCKFISH MAW

Clean the Maw (stomach) thoroughly in warm water. Make a forcemeat dressing with ¼ pound pork, 1 teaspoon butter, 1 egg, thyme, parsley and salt. Mix together with breadcrumbs. Stuff the Maw ¾ full, tie and simmer slowly in a little water for 2 ½ hours. Slice and serve with its own gravy.

Strachey tells of using a flat-bottomed boat and fishing further out where they "daily hooked great store of many kinds, as excellent angelfish, salmon peal, bonitos, sting ray, cabally, snappers, hogfish, sharks, dogfish, pilchards, mullets and rockfish, of which be divers kinds. And of these our governor dried and salted and, barreling them up, brought to see five hundred; for he had procured salt to be made with some brine which happily was preserved, and once having made a little quantity, he kept three or four pots boiling and two or three men attending nothing else". Fish nets were also used to catch up to 5,000 fish at a time. And they talk of finding crayfish "oftentimes greater than any of our best English lobsters" and crabs, oysters and whelks. "I think no island in the world may have greater store or better fish". Fish has always been important in Bermudian diets even though today we do not have it in such abundance.

In the olden days fishermen went through the islands blowing a conch shell to let everyone know they were coming. A fish was chosen, paid for and the fishermen strung it on a palmetto leaf for the buyer. Nowadays one goes to the flagpole on Front Street or to another dock and waits for the fishing boats to come in. It must be admitted that they are rather erratic as to hours ... one may come in, or two or three, or none at all. Until recently you were handed your fish or lobster on a string but now the fishermen have plastic bags. There is no fresh fish market as such, although frozen or an occasional fresh fish may be bought in grocery stores.

Bermudian fish receipts are endless and will be found throughout this book. Depending upon the fish, it can be fried, boiled, baked, stewed, steamed or grilled. Nothing is wasted as the fins and heads are used to make fish chowder.

YACHT CLUB FISH CHOWDER

Put into a stock pot: fish heads, fish fins, marrow bones and half a calves-head. Add 6 hard-boiled eggs, 2 large cans tomatoes, 2 pounds fried onions and chopped carrots, turnips, potatoes, thyme and parsley to taste. Boil on a slow fire for six hours then put through strainer. Put back on fire and add 1 bottle 'fino palma' sherry, 1 glass Barbados rum, 1 large bottle Bovril, 1 large bottle tomato ketchup, Worcestershire sauce to taste and butter. Pass black rum and sherry peppers when serving.

The Bermudian lobsters are actually spiny lobsters: they have no claws. They are prepared in the traditional ways: on the half-shell with drawn butter, cold with mayonnaise, Newburgh, Thermidor and in soups.

BAILEY'S BAY LOBSTER SOUP

Chop fine the meat of one small cooked lobster. Mix with it three crackers rolled fine, butter the size of an egg, salt, pepper and a speck of cayenne. Add gradually one pint of boiling milk, stirring all the while. Boil up once and serve.

Sir George Somers and his people also found an abundance of turtles and wild hogs ... probably hogs that had swum ashore from a previous shipwreck. Hunting parties set out with the ship's dog and brought back up to fifty live boars, sows and piglets in a week. These were kept in sties and fed berries from the cedars and palmettos. When the weather was too bad for fishing, hogs were eaten.

Seeing that the hogs thrived on the PALMETTO berries these were tried and liked by the castaways also. In fact they were found to be so good that they were eaten instead of bread, and the flour and meal could be saved to carry to Virginia. The palmetto was very useful as the leaves were used to thatch the cabins and the soft top was roasted and stewed, being very much like cabbage but better. As Strachey says, "they eat like cabbages, but not so offensively thankful (flatulent) to the stomach". He also writes of the palmetto fruit: "They bear a kind of berry, black and round, as big as a damson, which about December were ripe and luscious; being scaled whilst they are green, they eat like bullaces" (a variety of plum). Later settlers found that by taking the sap from the palmetto tree and fermenting it a highly intoxicating beverage could be made. In fact so many difficulties arose because of this "bibbey", as it was called, that it was banned. Tapping the palmetto for sap killed it, as did cutting the tender heart.

Another fruit found growing in abundance was "full of many sharp subtle pricks which we therefore called the prickle pear, the outside green, but, being opened, of a deep murrey, full of juice like a mulberry and just of the same substance and taste; we both eat them raw and baked". A candy was later made from these PRICKLY PEARS. They still grow along roadsides and in gardens, but are found to be more decorative than edible.

Bermuda was covered with CEDAR trees until a blight in the 1940s killed them. The early settlers found that by "seething, straining, and letting stand some three or four days, (the cedar berries) made a kind of pleasant drink". The dried sap was chewed with relish by children.

SEASIDE or BAY GRAPES were found growing along the southern shores. Their purple berries grow in bunches and although acrid in taste make good jellies.

BAY GRAPE JELLY

Use equal amounts of green and ripe Bay Grapes. Mash and boil until tender. Press out all the juice and strain through cheese cloth. Add 1 cup sugar to 1 cup of juice. Boil together about 20 minutes, skimming well. Pour into sterilized jars while warm.

In the winter when berries were scarce and the hogs became too lean they resorted to the turtles. These were baked or roasted to feed the company. "One turtle feasted well a dozen messes, appointing six to every mess". (One of these turtles fed more people than three hogs). Turtle eggs were also found to be delicious with the result that today there are very few turtles left and there is a temporary ban on catching them.

There was also an abundance of fowl: robins, white and grey heronshaws, bitterns, teals, snipes, crows, hawks, cormorants, bald coots, moor hens, owls and bats. One of the most unusual birds found was the cahow which only came out of the rocks to feed at night. It made strange noises, almost howling. These birds were probably responsible for the tales of weird noises recounted by early sailors. The shipwrecked company found them delicious. "Our men found a pretty way to take them, which was by standing on the rocks or sands by the seaside and hollowing, laughing, and making the strangest outcry that possibly they could. With the noise whereof the birds would come flocking to that place and settle upon the very arms and head of him that so cried, and still creep nearer and nearer, answering the noise themselves; by which our men would weigh them with their hands, and which weighed heaviest they took for the best and left the others alone. And so our men would take twenty dozen in two hours of the chiefest of them; and they were a good and well-relished fowl, fat and full as a partridge. In January we had great store of their eggs, which are as great as an hen's egg, and so fashioned and white shelled, and have no difference in yolk nor white from an hen's egg". Unfortunately these thousands of birds have almost completely disappeared. The cahows were thought to be extinct until 1906 when a few were rediscovered and now all efforts are being made to help them re-establish themselves.

Sir George Somers planted the first Bermudian garden near Gates Bay in August of the arrival of the Sea 'Venture. For though there was plenty of fish, fowl and pork the bay grapes, cedar berries, palmetto and prickly pears were the only edible plants. He sowed muskmelons, peas, onions, radishes, lettuces and many other English seeds and kitchen herbs that he had had on board ship. These came up quickly but were eaten as quickly by birds and hogs.

On August 28, 1609, eight men left in the Sea 'Venture's longboat that had been covered, but they were never seen again. Work was then started on a ship to take the survivors on to Jamestown. The Deliverance was completed in March, 1610 and a smaller ship, Patience, was finished in May. Both set off on Thursday, May 10, 1610, filled with salted meat, tortoise oil and other provisions for their trip. Two deserters, Carter and Edwards, stayed behind. The ships reached Jamestown in less than two weeks to find desolation and only 60 survivors of the original 500 settlers. Sir George Somers decided to return to Bermuda for food for the impoverished Jamestowners and boarded the Patience with a small crew and set sail. He was never to return to Virginia for he died soon after his arrival in Bermuda and his body was taken back to England. This time three men were left behind: Carter, Waters and Chard. These were "The Three Kings of Bermuda" about whom Washington Irving wrote.

The next Bermudian garden was planted by these three men. When Governor Richard Moore arrived with settlers in Bermuda on board the *Plough* in July 1612 he found Chard, Waters and Carter in good health. And they had an acre of corn ready to be harvested, pumpkins, Indian beans and wheat. There was also a supply of tortoises and salt pork. The ship *Elizabeth* brought planting potatoes later in the year. And "in this ship was brought the first potato-roots, which flourished exceedingly for a time, till by negligence they were almost lost (all but two castaway roots) that have so wonderfully increased, they are a maine releef to all the inhabitants". It is interesting to note that the first potatoes cultivated in America came from Bermuda. Potatoes and fish have long been important Bermudian staples. This is reflected in old parish doggerel: "All the way to Bailey's Bay, Fish and taters every day".

Governor Daniel Tucker arrived in Bermuda in 1616 as the first governor under the Bermuda Company. The shareholders in the company wanted Bermuda to grow vegetables and fruits that would be of use in England and in return they would supply the needs of these first settlers. Governor Tucker brought an abundance of seeds with him along with instructions on how to cultivate them. An interesting passage in his instructions reads: "If your season after sowing be too dry for want of rain you must water with fresh water, for which purpose we have sent you two watering pots, which we pray you let be used as well for your vines and seeds and other plants." Anis, fennel, marjoram, basil, onion, mulberry, orange, lemon and citron were sown and vines were planted. A Mr. Wilmott was sent to the Savage Islands (West Indies) for cattle, cassava, sugar-canes, figs, pineapples, plantains (bananas) and papayas (pawpaws).

CASSAVA is the West Indian name for the starch found in the roots of the "Manihot utilissima". Its juice is used for making cassareepe, a preservative and flavouring that is used in making Pepper Pot. Tapioca is also prepared from it. It was seriously cultivated in 1619 for it was hoped that it would be a profitable crop. The Reverend Lewis Hughes, first minister appointed to Bermuda by the Virginia Company (1612) wrote this about the cassava root: "The Casaua roote is like to proue a great blessing of God unto you, because it makes as fine white bread as can be made of wheat, and (as I am persuaded) wholesome because the Indians that liue of it are tall and strong men." He then gave a receipt for cassava bread. This is believed to be the oldest Bermudian receipt.

"HOW TO MAKE BREAD OF CASAVA ROOTES"

First wash, and scrape cleane, or pare away the out-side. Then grate the root upon a Grater, as you do bread: get Graters made of purpose, with holes somewhat bigger than ordinary. If you want a Grater, you may make shift with a rough pumish stone, whereof you may finde some upon the Bayes of the Sea side, or with nayles broad pointed, driven thick through bord.

Presse out the juice through a Bagge of haire, as you doe Ver juice; then spread the grated roote upon a cleane cloath in the Sunne to dry.

That which will not goe through the Sive, beat in a Morter till it be small like meale, and sift it againe.

Take the sifted roote, and strew it in a cleane dripping panne, and put it into the Oven, and it will bake in a quater of an houre. The oven must not be too hot.

You must not knead the roote, as you doe Dowe, nor put water to it, but strew it dry, like Saw-dust, almost an inch thicke.

If you have no Oven, you may bake it on a Trivet or three stones, with a little fire, if you make a great fire, it will not bake, but crumble like Saw-dust: remember to turne it three or four times, unless you bake it in a Oven, then it needes no turning.

This recipe was given to the St George's Historical Society by Wesley Frank Craven, assistant Professor of History, New York University.

Lady Butterfield gave us the following recipe for West Indian Pepper Pot. A special earthen pot was brought to Bermuda from the West Indies to cook it in.

WEST INDIAN PEPPER POT

Put one large pint of warm water in a bowl. Add 1 tablespoon of brown sugar, 1 teaspoon salt and ½ teacup of cassareepe. Stir until dissolved. Put into the earthen pot: 2 thick fresh pork chops that have been browned and cut into thin pieces, 1 sliced raw ox-tail, 2 cooked pigs feet, 1 cut up old fowl (raw) and as many bird peppers to taste or cayenne pepper. Pour liquid over all and cook for three days before using. Stir with a long-handled wooden spoon. Heat up and boil every day to keep from turning sour. You can put in cooked beef or even fresh pork, but never put vegetables or fish. Stir often. Keep all the bones in the pot. Do not open pot too often and cook over a slow fire. Serve hot over rice.

Unfortunately the cultivation of Governor Tucker's plants was not successful because they were devoured by rats. The plague of rats was so bad that settlers stopped coming out from England. And food was in great demand. Most Bermudians lived on a restricted diet of salt and smoked meats, fish and hardy staples like pumpkins, sweet potatoes, turnips, carrots and pawpaws. An occasional whale or turtle meant a feast. Cooking was done in open fireplaces and the baking in brick ovens. Here is an old receipt for pumpkin stew.

PUMPKIN STEW

Line a black gypsy pot with pastry. Put in cut up pumpkin, potatoes, salt pork or beef, with plenty of seasonings. Cover with pastry and cook over a cedar fire.

PUMPKIN is one of Bermuda's most important summer and autumn crops and is used as a vegetable or as a sweet.

EMILY PUGH'S PUMPKIN FRITTERS

¼ pound flour
¼ pound sugar
 1 egg
½ pint milk
 1 pound cooked pumpkin
¼ teaspoon cinnamon

Beat until stiff, drop in a very hot pan and cook until brown.

PUMPKIN SEED CANDY

Dry pumpkin seeds in the oven, cool and dip in black molasses.

At the end of the 17th century Bermudians were whaling, fishing, salt raking at Turks Island and ship-building. All of this helped the economy but farming was neglected. Most food and supplies had to be brought from America.

Cultivation of citrus trees, mulberries, pawpaws and pineapples was tried again but was not successful because of mildew. Corn, potatoes, cabbages and onions were the most successful crops. Trading developed with the West Indies, Newfoundland and America. Bermuda supplied stone, salt, cedar, palmetto goods and whale oil in exchange for dry goods, rum and sugar. (However, many Bermudians could not afford to buy even the available flour, corn or rice.)

RUM is still a favourite in Bermuda and many interesting drinks have been concocted.

BERMUDA SHRUB

("Shrub" is derived from the Arabic "Shrub" meaning a drink or draught.)

1 gallon old rum (Demarara)
6 pounds sugar (white or brown)
3 pints orange juice (sour Bermuda oranges)
1 ounce green ginger, grated
1 nutmeg, grated
1 teaspoon cloves, powdered
3 pints boiling water

Dissolve 3 pounds sugar in 1 quart rum (Demarara is black rum) and add orange juice, ginger, cloves and nutmeg. Add the other 3 quarts of rum and stir well. To the 3 pints boiling water add 3 pounds sugar and let boil about 10 minutes. Then add the other ingredients and stir well. Let stand, covered, one week, strain through cheese cloth and bottle. "The older it is the better."

BERMUDA MILK PUNCH

18 lemons, preferably thick-skinned
1 gallon old rum (Demarara)
4 pounds white sugar
4 quarts boiling water
2 quarts boiling milk

Peel lemons as thinly as possible, take no white. Steep the peelings in 2 quarts of rum. Squeeze the juice of the lemons on the sugar. Set aside covered for 3 days, then mix together. Add the remaining rum, the boiling water, and lastly the boiling milk. Let stand all night, then strain through a double-flannel jelly bag. Let everything go in the bag and remain till the end of the straining. The first that goes through will have to go back several times till perfectly clear.

BERMUDA RUM SWIZZLE

6 ounces Barbados or Jamaica rum (light brown in colour)
2 ounces Demarara rum (black)
1 ounce apricot brandy (optional)
juice of 4 limes or lemons
1½ ounces honey, sugar syrup or Falernum
4 dashes bitters

Pour all ingredients into a pitcher and add crushed ice. Churn vigorously with a "swizzle-stick" until a frothing head appears. Strain into a cocktail glass. (Lady Brassey described "swizzle-sticks" in 1883 as being "cut from some kind of creeper, close to a joint, where four or five shoots branch out at right angles so as to produce a star-like circle." Rotated between the palms of the hands it mixes and froths the drink. Sterling silver "swizzle-sticks" are also available.)

Bermudians took salt to Newfoundland for salting codfish and then took salt cod to the West Indies. Some of the salt cod found its way to Bermuda and thus became the main ingredient in the traditional Bermudian breakfast, "codfish and bananas". A receipt for this is given further on.

In 1839 Governor William Reid imported two farmers from England as well as the latest farming equipment. Citrus, pawpaws and bananas became plentiful. ARROWROOT was being successfully cultivated by the mid-1800s and exported. Bermudian arrowroot was acclaimed to be the finest in the world and the Camden mark on arrowroot bags was world famous. However with mass production, the arrowroot quality deteriorated and the industry was lost. Except for a few plants in private gardens it is no longer grown.

ARROWROOT PUDDING

4 tablespoons Bermudian arrowroot
1 quart milk
1 tablespoon butter
4 eggs
4 tablespoons sugar
Vanilla or lemon flavouring to taste

Damp the arrowroot with a little cold milk, add butter and well-beaten eggs. Sweeten the milk and bring to a boil, pour over the arrowroot and other ingredients. Stir well, add flavouring and turn into a buttered pudding dish. Bake in a moderate oven.

By the late 1800s early potatoes, onions, celery, tomatoes and parsley were being exported to New York during the winter and spring months. Portuguese farmers from the Azores were brought in and farming was developed on a large scale. Ships began arriving regularly from America and with these ships came the winter tourists and the beginning of Bermuda's main livelihood.

Bermuda still imports most everything including all meat and a large quantity of vegetables. A large variety of vegetables and fruits are grown for domestic use but the quantity is often insufficient. Many families have vegatable gardens and with time and space interesting vegetables may be grown. A few of the lesser known vegetables that grow well are: celeriac, sweet fennel, Jerusaleum artichokes, oyster plants, sorrel, corn salad, endive and artichokes.

Cassava is still cultivated for domestic use as it is the basic ingredient in the traditional Bermudian Christmas dish: Cassava Pie. Christmas dinner wouldn't be Christmas dinner for "Mudians" without this delicacy and there are as many receipts for it as there are Bermudian families. (Receipts are given in the last chapter.) No one knows who made the first cassava pie but as the first settlers were English it was natural to make a "meat pasty" using local ingredients of cassava, poultry, pork and eggs. The preparation is rather long and complicated as a two year old root has to be dug, soaked, scraped and grated. The grated pulp is then squeezed as the juice is poisonous. Frozen prepared cassava is also available.

Some of the excitement of making Cassava Pie has been lost with the coming of modern conveniences such as the refrigerator and electric and gas ovens. There was such a danger of spoilage of the meats that one old cook book concluded with an antidote for ptomaine poisoning. And our modern ovens have replaced the old brick ovens that were heated with cedar until glowing, the coals raked out and the pies shoved in with a palmetto leaf poker. How excited the children must have been when the small sample pie was ready to be tasted! Cassava Pie is eaten any time of the day or night all during Christmas week, some is even frozen to bring out at Easter and Cup Match (annual cricket matches between Somerset and St George's teams).

Helen M. Fessenden describes a Christmas dinner in the late 1800s as a time of "fine and confused feeding". After church there was a huge family dinner on a long table with a "stately array of silver and napery and beautiful with flowers and bowls of apples, oranges, nuts and raisins that might well have come from fairyland." The menu included: soup, turkey (20 pounds), sweet and white potatoes, salad, jellies, floating island, custards, and a flaming plum pudding. Port and sherry wines were passed during the meal. Needless to say why this grace was found appropriate:

"The Lord be praised, my tummy's raised
An inch above the table,
And I be damned but I be crammed
As full as I be able."

The day after Christmas is still a holiday in the English tradition and called "Boxing Day". (Thus called because gifts were distributed to tradesmen, public servants, etc). And it is the day that the Gombey dancers make their appearance. They are a strange mixture of English Christmas Mummers and African and Indian dancers. Always exciting with their brightly coloured costumes, masks, plumed head-dresses and exotic music. In the late 1800s there was horse racing at Shelly Bay on Boxing Day and families gathered there with picnics. These were usually leftovers from Christmas dinner: cold sliced cassava pie, ham and turkey. Lemonade, rum punch, mineral water and homemade ginger-beer were the popular beverages. Here is an old receipt for ginger-beer.

GINGER BEER

1 pound green ginger, washed, beaten and boiled
7 pounds white sugar
6 lemons, juice and skins

Add enough boiling water to make five gallons. When cool, add half a yeast cake, shake well and leave standing for 24 hours before bottling. Mix above either in a stone jar or wooden keg. Have new corks for your bottles and tie down with twine.

New Year's Day menus always include "Peas and Plenty" for who doesn't believe that "the more whole grains you eat on New Year's Day, the more happy days (or days of plenty) you will have"?

PEAS AND PLENTY

Wash, sort and soak overnight one pound of Blackeyed Peas. The next day, bring the peas to a boil in 2 quarts salted water. Add sprigs of parsley and thyme. Add one chopped onion and squares of salt pork. Then add 2 cups rice. Cook until thick. The rice may be omitted and just before serving, add boiled sweet potatoes or dumplings.

Telephones came into use in 1887 and "central" was everyone's friend. Terry Tucker tells the story of the housewife in Somerset who is reputed to have rung "central" everytime she put eggs on to boil and "central" would call her back in three minutes to tell her when they were done. Electricity was first used in 1904. There is an ad in the Royal Gazette, 1921, for electric fans and ranges.

Fresh water has always been scarce in Bermuda for there are no rivers or springs. We are dependent on rain water. Rev. Hughes wrote of the "ponds and welles of very good and holsome water". And to supplement these we now have a distillation plant. All houses in Bermuda have a water tank and rain water flows from the whitewashed roofs into it. These tanks hold from 10 to 20 thousand gallons.

CORN along with potatoes for a long time formed the staple food for the island. In the 1600s it was stored in the forts ... as much as 300,000 ears at a time ... and renewed annually to guard against scarcity. It was prepared by pounding in a mortar with a pestle. One governor is said to have complained to the Bermuda Company that instead of keeping their muskets in good working order the men used them as pestles for pounding corn. Corn was exported to the West Indies and also sold to vessels touching Bermuda for supplies.

Here are some very old receipts for using corn:

MISS PATTY'S CORN BROTH

1 pint grits, ¼ pound pork, 1 old fowl, cover with water and boil for 3 hours.

TUSCARORA

Corn-meal mush thinned to a gruel consistency, sweetened, served hot with a little rum added was a very satisfying night-cap among the working class in the old days.

INDIAN POUND CAKE

8 eggs, weight of eggs in sugar, weight of six of them in corn meal, (half a pound of meal), ½ pound butter, 1 large nutmeg.

Sift dry ingredients into a bowl, add egg and milk, stirring lightly. Fold in melted butter. Bake in an 8-inch square pan at 425° F. for 20 to 25 minutes.

From those first orange and lemon seeds of 1616 the cultivation has spread to encompass a large variety of citrus. In the late 1600s there was such an abundance of oranges that they were one of Bermuda's principal exports.

In 1621 the governor, Captain Nathaniel Butler sent two chests to Virginia filled with "figs, pomgranats, oranges, lemons, sugar canes, plantanes, potatoes, pawpaws, cassado roots, red pepper and prickell pear". A ship soon came from Virginia with thanks and a supply of "aquavitae, Oile, Sacke and Bricks in exchange of more Fruits and Plants (including 20,000 weight of Potatoes), Ducks, Turkies and Limestone". Then the first governor of the Massachusetts Bay, John Winthrop, (1630-49), writes of receiving on the ship Rebecca "30,000 weight of potatoes and store of oranges and limes which were a great relief to our people".

Even rents were paid in oranges ... In 1634 Governor Woodhouse leased land and the rent was 100 oranges, 100 lemons and 100 potatoes. It is said that incoming ships could smell oranges blossoms as far as 30 miles out at sea. And there is an advertisement in the Royal Gazette (November 14,

1855) signed William B. Perot offering from 15 to 20 thousand sweet oranges for sale from the citrus grove at Par-la-Ville.

Unfortunately, in the 1800s the trees were attacked by fruit flies, scale and diseases. Hundreds of fruit trees were lost for ways of combatting the pests were unknown. Under the direction of Mr. St. George Butterfield, chairman of the Board of Agriculture, many citrus trees were imported from Florida in the late 1940s and early 50s. A wide variety of ORANGES, LEMONS, LIMES, GRAPEFRUITS and other citrus is now cultivated. Bermudian housewives made excellent jams with these fruits as well as other dishes.

BERMUDA SOUR ORANGE MARMALADE

Allow 1 quart of water to 3 oranges. Cut thin and remove seeds. Soak for 24 hours. Then boil till tender. Next day: measure fruit and to each pound of pulp allow 1½ pounds sugar. Boil 20 minutes after it starts to boil. If not firm enough when tested, boil a little longer. Bottle and seal.

LEMON CURD

1 cup margarine
10 eggs
4 cups sugar
½ teaspoon salt
grated rind of 5 lemons
1½ cups lemon juice

Combine the first 5 ingredients in top of double boiler and cook over hot water, stirring constantly until the margarine has melted. Then add the lemon juice and cook until the mixture thickens, about 20 minutes. Stir constantly. Do not boil. Pour into hot sterilized jars and seal. Store in cool place. This may be used hot as a lemon sauce or cooled as a filling for cakes, pies or tarts.

THREE FRUIT MARMALADE

3 large oranges
1 large grapefruit
3 lemons
sugar

1st day: cut ends off fruit, slice very thinly and then chop finely. To every cup of fruit add 3 cups water. Soak 24 hours.
2nd day: bring to a boil and allow to boil for 10-15 minutes. Set aside.

19

3rd day: to every cup of fruit and liquid add a cup of sugar. Bring to a boil and cook until it jellies. Pour into sterlized jars and seal.

LEMON NUT BREAD

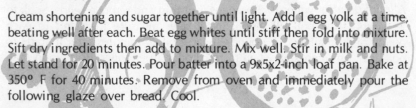

⅓ cup shortening
1 cup sugar
2 eggs, separated
1 ⅔ cups flour
2 teaspoons baking powder
½ teaspoon salt
grated rind of 1 lemon
1 cup milk
½ cup chopped walnuts

Cream shortening and sugar together until light. Add 1 egg yolk at a time, beating well after each. Beat egg whites until stiff then fold into mixture. Sift dry ingredients then add to mixture. Mix well. Stir in milk and nuts. Let stand for 20 minutes. Pour batter into a 9x5x2-inch loaf pan. Bake at 350° F for 40 minutes. Remove from oven and immediately pour the following glaze over bread. Cool.

Glaze:

Stir ⅓ cup sugar into the juice of 1 lemon and let stand until dissolved.

ORANGE BISCUITS

Take the grated rind of an orange, six fresh eggs, a quarter of a pound of flour, and three quarters of a pound of powdered lump sugar; put these into a mortar, beat them to a paste. Put the paste into cases, and bake it in the same way as biscuits.

CALAMONDINE MARMALADE

4 pounds calamondines
9 ½ pounds sugar
10 pints water and 1 pint lemon juice
    or
12 pints water

Cut up fruit and remove seeds. Cook in water until soft. Then add sugar and stir until dissolved.(Put silver dollar or spoon in pan to keep marmalade from burning).Boil for 1 ½ hours or until reaches soft ball stage. Pour into sterilized jars and seal. (The calamondine is a small fruit, a cross between a mandarine and a kumquat).

An old almanac found in the St. George's Historical Museum dated 1736 was filled with handwritten receipts. One of these was for Orange Cakes.

ORANGE CAKE
[1736]

Take a pound of Seville Oranges, cut them in quarters, and put the pulp and juice into a basin, then mince the skins as small as you can and put them in a marble mortar. Add a pound and quarter of fine loaf sugar, beat fine and sifted, beat these well together, then put in the pulp and juice with two spoonfuls of lemon juice taking care not to put in any pips, mix all these well together and drop it in dishes rubbed with butter and set them before the fire but not too near. When they are candied at the top, turn them with a knife. They must be quite hard dried or they will not keep.

Other receipts using citrus will be found throughout this book.

GUAVA trees are occasionally found in private gardens. A delicious jelly can be made from the ripened fruit.

NELLIE'S GUAVA JELLY

Cut the guavas in two, do not peel, cover well with water and boil until like jelly. Strain. Cool. To a pint of liquid add a pound of sugar, one or two drops of lime or lemon juice. Boil until it jellies. Guava jelly is an important ingredient in Bermuda Syllabub.

BERMUDA SYLLABUB
(from the Bermuda Historical Society cook book, 1932)

1 teaspoonful of sugar, 1 teaspoonful guava jelly, enough Marsala wine to cover jelly. Top with whipped cream. Serve in tall glasses.

Another receipt for "syllabub" was found in an almanac dated 1736.

EVERLASTING SYLLABUB

To 5 gills of cream put a pound of double refined sugar beat and sifted. Grate the rind of 3 lemons and squeeze the juice into a pint of Lisbon (port) and ½ a pint of Mountain Wine. Put altogether and whisk it ½ an hour, then fill your glasses. It will keep 8 or 10 days.

No cook book on Bermuda would be complete without recipes for using BANANAS. What does one do with 500 ripe bananas? Quite often it seems as though they ripen overnight. Large quantities are eaten freshly picked as they have a most agreeable flavour. And through the years numerous receipts have been developed to use them to advantage. The most common banana grown in Bermuda comes from the Canary Islands, "Musa Cavendishii". An interesting historical sidelight is that the first bananas to be exhibited in England came from Bermuda. A Thomas John exhibited a bunch in his apothecary shop before 1644. Bananas ripen all year long and are the chief fruit crop of the island.

BANANA BREAD

1½ cups sifted flour
1 teaspoon salt
1 teaspoon baking soda
⅓ cup shortening
¾ cup light brown sugar
2 eggs
1 cup mashed bananas
½ cup milk
½ cup chopped walnuts (optional)

Sift dry ingredients together. Cream sugar and shortening thoroughly. Add the eggs, one at a time, beating well after each addition. Then add mashed bananas and beat mixture till light. Add dry ingredients alternately with the milk, beating well after each addition. Beat until smooth. Stir in walnuts. Pour batter into well greased 9-inch by 5-inch by 2-inch loaf pan. Bake at 350° F for one hour and 5 minutes. Allow to cool for 10 minutes in pan, then remove to rack. (Banana bread freezes quite well).

HEAVENLY BANANA PIE

3 medium bananas
2 egg whites
1 cup powdered sugar
¼ teaspoon salt
½ teaspoon lemon juice
chopped nuts, whipped cream

Force bananas through a sieve, add unbeaten egg whites, sugar, salt and lemon juice. Beat thoroughly until light and fluffy. Pour in a pastry shell and bake in a very moderate oven (325° F) for twenty or thirty minutes. When cold serve with whipped cream sprinkled with chopped nuts.

BANANA CUSTARD
(from the Royal Gazette, 1918)

1 ¼ cups milk
1 egg, beaten
1 tablespoon flour
¼ cup Bermuda honey
2 ripe bananas
⅛ teaspoon salt
½ teaspoon vanilla

Dissolve the flour in ¼ cup of milk. Heat the remainder of the milk and add the flour. Cook until slightly thickened. Add the honey, salt, vanilla, egg and the bananas cut in thin slices. Pour in glasses and chill.

BANANA CHUTNEY

1 pound onions, chopped
8 bananas, sliced
½ pound dates, chopped
1 ½ cups vinegar
2 teaspoons ginger
¾ cup raisins
1 teaspoon salt
1 teaspoon curry
2 cups water
1 cup sugar

Simmer first four ingredients for 20 minutes in a covered pan. Add the rest of the ingredients and boil uncovered until mixture thickens. Bottle and seal.

FLAMING BANANAS

6 medium-ripe bananas
2 tablespoons butter
½ cup lime or lemon juice
½ cup sugar
½ cup black rum

Melt butter in skillet. Add bananas cut in half lengthwise. Sauté over high heat until browned, turn once. Combine lime juice and sugar and pour over bananas. Cook two minutes. Pour over rum, remove from heat and flame. (½ cup raisins may be added if desired).

Tea parties have always been a favourite way of entertaining friends. Mrs William Zuill recited an amusing verse about these:

"Oh, how pleasant 'tis to see
our dear relations come to tea,
But better still, it is to know
That when they've had their tea they'll go."

After the introduction of tennis in Bermuda in 1873 tennis tea parties were in vogue. Miss Gladys Hutchings, the first Bermudian to play at Wimbledon, tells of a typical tennis tea party of the '20s or earlier. The players (10 to 12) arrived about 2.30, some on bicycles (cars were not allowed until 1946) others in carriages. The ladies were always dressed in white with coloured sweaters and lovely homespun coats to match. The men wore long white flannels. Then later, guests invited to look on arrived. About 4.30 everyone was invited to have tea around the dining table which was beautifully set with flowers matching the tea set. What a spread! Sandwiches galore (nut or brown bread), hot biscuits or Johnny Cake, cookies, layer cakes (lemon, orange, chocolate, cocoanut). (Bermuda's moist climate is said to be good for making layer cakes). Many cups of tea were consumed, the men usually had up to six. This was a wonderful way of entertaining. Some days the standard of tennis on the grass courts was high but other days of the "Hit, miss and giggle" type. All great fun!

Here is an old Bailey's Bay cake receipt of the late Mrs W.B. Smith served at the Bailey's Bay Tennis Club on their Club Day.

COCOANUT LAYER CAKE

4 eggs, separated
2 cups sugar
¾ cup water
2 cups flour
2 teaspoons baking powder
flavour to taste

Beat till light the egg yolks. Add sugar gradually and mix till it is well creamed. Add the water. Measure 2 cups of sifted flour, mix in baking powder and resift it. Add to the above mixture.

Whip till light the egg whites, then fold them lightly into the batter. Add flavouring. (Grated lemon rind is good.)

Bake cake in two layer tins (well greased) in a moderate oven (325° F) for about half an hour. When the cake is cool, spread between the layers and on top with a white icing. Sprinkle the top of each layer with grated fresh (or tinned) cocoanut.

BERMUDA JOHNNY BREAD

¼ cup sugar
1½ cups flour
¼ cup butter
1 egg
½ cup milk
¼ teaspoon salt
2 teaspoons baking powder

Mix dry ingredients, cut in butter till coarse crumbs. Measure milk, add egg and beat slightly. Add to dry ingredients. Roll out on floured board to ½ inch thickness, then cut in rounds. Bake on well buttered griddle, medium heat, turning once. (Johnny Bread was originally called Journey Bread because it was found to keep better on board ship than regular bread).

TEA SCONES

2 ounces margarine
8 ounces self-rising flour
1 handful sultanas
a little sour milk

Mix to a smooth paste and drop by spoonfuls on greased baking sheet. Bake about ten minutes in quick oven.

HERMITS
("Small cakes dear to our grandmother's heart.")

To 2 scant cupfuls of sugar add one of butter, one of sweet milk, three heaping cups of flour, and three eggs, whites and yolks beaten separately. To the milk when it is measured out stir a half teaspoonful of soda. For flavouring add two teaspoonfuls of cinnamon, a half teaspoonful of cloves, a little nutmeg, a cup of raisins, seeded and chopped, and a cup of English walnuts, chopped finely, ½ cup of currants, washed, dried and dredged with a little of the flour. Do not roll out, but drop the mixture in tablespoonfuls on buttered tins allowing space between for the spreading. This makes uneven, rather ragged looking little cakes whose toothsomeness, however, compensates for any lack of symmetry.

ORANGE MARMALADE CAKE

¾ cup shortening
1¾ cups sugar
3 eggs
grated rind of 1 orange

½ cup orange juice
1 tablespoon lemon juice
½ cup cold water
3 cups sifted flour
4 teaspoons baking powder
¾ teaspoon salt

Cream shortening and sugar until fluffy. Then add 1 egg at a time beating well after each. Beat in next 3 ingredients. Sift dry ingredients together and add to mixture alternately with the water, ending with flour. Line 2 9-inch cake pans with wax paper, then pour in batter. Bake at 375° F for 30 minutes. Allow to cool in pans for 10 minutes, then remove to rack.

Filling:
Mix 1¼ cups orange marmalade with 1 cup of chopped nuts (walnuts). Spread between layers.

Frosting:
1½ cups sugar
2 egg whites
⅓ cup orange juice
1 teaspoon orange rind

Place all ingredients in top of double boiler over boiling water and beat for 7 minutes. Remove from heat and continue beating until frosting holds its shape. Frost sides and top of cake and decorate with candied orange peel.

Candied Orange Peel:
Cut orange peel in lengthwise sections, cover with water and bring to a boil. Reduce heat and cook till soft, about 15-20 minutes. Drain, then scrape out white part and cut peel into thin strips. Bring to a boil 1 cup of sugar and ½ cup water, add 1 cup of prepared peel. Cook over low heat till transparent. Spread on a plate to cool. Roll in granulated sugar and allow to dry. Store in an air-tight jar.

Lemonade and tamarind beverages were also served. Mrs Charles Burland's receipt for Tamarind Beverage follows:

TAMARIND BEVERAGE

Boil together equal quantity of shelled Tamarinds and brown sugar with a little water for about ten to fifteen minutes. Bottle when cool. To prepare for drinking, put a reasonable quantity in a jug, add water and stir well. A little lemon juice and rind may be added if desired.

Everyone has heard of Bermuda ONIONS and one of the nicknames for Bermudians is "onions". The Bermudian soil and climate are well-adapted to growing a fine quality of early onion with a delicate flavour. Onions were cultivated on a large scale in the mid-1800s and many were shipped to the West Indies as early as the 17th century. In 1899 well over 400,000 boxes were exported. At one time baskets were woven from palmetto leaves for shipping onions. The first Bermuda onions sold in New York (1856) were packed in palmetto baskets. Here is a favourite receipt for small onions.

PICKLED BERMUDA ONIONS

Peel carefully small onions and leave in salted water for 48 hours. Change the brine and let them remain in it for another 48 hours. Wipe the onions dry, place in bottles with mixed whole spices. Boil your vinegar, a few drops of sweet oil put in the vinegar before cooking well prevent any film from forming on it. When lukewarm, pour the vinegar over the onions, cork tightly.

Until recent years one of the traditional Bermudian celebrations was Guy Fawkes Day, November 5. The discovery of the gunpowder plot in London was celebrated by fireworks displays and the burning in effigy of Guy Fawkes sporting a pumpkin or calabash head. Everyone then went home to eat sweet potato pudding and drink cedar berry wine. In the Bermudian records of 1621 it says, "the damnable plot of the powder treason was solemnized, with praises, sermons, and a great feast, where to the governor invited the Chiefs of the Spaniards, where drinking the king's health, it was honoured with a quick volley of small shot ... neither was the afternoon without musike and dancing, and at night many huge bone-fires of sweet wood".

SWEET POTATO PUDDING

3 pounds sweet potatoes, boiled and mashed
3 pounds sweet potatoes, grated raw
2 tablespoons butter
1½ tablespoons lard
1 egg
a little salt
sweeten to taste, brown sugar preferred
4 bananas, mashed
Flavour with allspice and grated orange or lemon peel
Flour to bind.
Place in a greased baking pan about 1½ inches thick, mark with end of spoon and bake in hot oven.

Bermudian weddings ... what happy occasions! ... loved by all. In true Bermudian fashion the bride and her attendants arrive at the flower - decorated church in horse-drawn carriages ... the coachmen wearing white suits and sun-helmets ... the horses and carriages decorated with white ribbons. After the cermony the bridal party returns to the bride's home for an enormous reception in the garden. Friends come from miles (all 20 of them) around to toast the newlyweds with witty speeches and champagne and rum punch. (In days gone by the women and children were served tea and soda pop and only the men rum punch).

Traditionally there are two cakes, one for the bride and one for the groom. The bride's cake is a three-tiered fruit cake covered with silver leaf symbolizing prosperity, surrounded with ivy ("I cling to thee") and tiny pink rose buds for love. A young cedar tree is on the top tier and is planted by the bride and groom during the reception. If it grows their love will grow ... and of course it always does! The groom's cake is a plain one-layer cake covered with gold leaf.

BRIDE'S SILVER WEDDING CAKE

This cake is always made weeks in advance and macerated in rum.

2 pounds raisins
1 large package of citron
2 blocks of dates
1 large package of glacé cherries

Chop and combine fruit, sprinkle with flour and set aside.

1 pound butter
1 pound sugar
1 dozen eggs, separated
1 pound flour
1 teaspoon baking powder
1 cup rum
1 tablespoon lemon juice
1 tablespoon vanilla

Cream butter and sugar till light. Add egg yolks one at a time, beating well after each. Sift flour and baking powder and add to butter mixture. Beat just till smooth. Stir in rum, lemon juice and vanilla. Beat egg whites till soft peaks form. Fold into batter. Stir in the fruit. Pour into a well greased, paper-lined bottom layer cake pan. For the second tier make ¾ of the above recipe and for the top tier make ½ of the recipe. Bake at 275° F. The bottom layer will take about 3½ hours and the second and third layers about 2 hours. Test for doneness with a straw or knitting needle. Permit the cakes to cool, then remove from pans. Wrap in rum soaked cheese cloth, cover with foil and leave in a cool place for several weeks.

GROOM'S GOLD WEDDING CAKE

1 pound butter
1 pound sugar
1 dozen eggs, separated
1 pound flour
1 teaspoon baking powder
1 tablespoon lemon juice
1 tablespoon vanilla

Prepare the batter as for the bride's cake, omitting the fruit and rum. Pour into a deep well greased, paper-lined cake pan. Bake at 275° F for about 1½ hours. Test for doneness.

A few days before the wedding the cakes are brought out to be iced. Both cakes are iced with white boiled icing and allowed to dry. Then comes the delicate operation of covering the cakes with gold and silver leaf. (This can be purchased in books at the pharmacy). This must take place in an absolutely airless room. Using a very fine artist's brush or feather, paint a small section of the cake with egg white, put the gold or silver leaf on top and gently pull off the paper backing. Continue to do this till the cakes are completely covered.

CHAMPAGNE PUNCH

Cover a half of a diced fresh pineapple, or a quart of fresh strawberries with 1½ cups of granulated sugar. Pour one wine glass of brandy and one bottle of Rhine wine over the fruit. Let it stand, tightly covered, from two to four hours. Immediately before serving, add ice cubes, a bottle of sparkling water and two bottles of well chilled champagne.

Strange as it may seem, these cakes are not cut at the reception but "substitute cakes", plain and fruit, are served to the guests along with small sandwiches. It is a custom in some families to save the top layer of the bride's cake and serve it at the christening of the first child. Around the turn of the century the bride's cake was served to friends at a special tea following the wedding trip. The wedding veil covered the tea table. Some couples have even kept part of their cake to serve at their 25th wedding anniversary. Receptions before the wedding used to be held at the groom's home for his friends but after several bridegrooms barely made it to the church, these were abandoned.

Many interesting fruits and vegetables grow practically wild. One of these can be eaten ripe as a melon, cooked green as a vegetable, used as a meat tenderizer, is rich in Vitamin C and is very decorative. This is, of course, the PAWPAW or more correctly called PAPAYA. The ripe fruit is delicious cut in half, seeds removed and sprinkled with lime juice. It is also a good addition to a fruit salad. Green it is excellent peeled and boiled and served with butter, a white sauce or cheese sauce. It jams well. It contains papaine, a digestive enzyme, that is the base for many commercial meat tenderizers. Bermudians have always known that a green pawpaw added to a stew makes even the toughest old rooster tender and its leaves act as a tenderizer when wrapped around lower cuts of meat. Juice from the green fruit is considered an effective vermifuge if taken on a lump of sugar before breakfast for three mornings. Warts were removed by dropping the juice on them and rheumatism was aided by applying the leaves to the affected area. The juice was even used to remove freckles! Children have been known to use the hollow leaf stalks as pea shooters.

PAWPAW CHUTNEY

2 pounds ripe pawpaw, cubed
½ pound grated apple
1 quart vinegar
½ package raisins
½ pound onions, chopped
½ teaspoon mustard
1 pound brown sugar
1 teaspoon peppercorns or allspice
1½ teaspoons salt
1 teaspoon curry
1 teaspoon ginger

Combine all ingredients and cook, stirring carefully, until thick. Pour into hot jars and seal.

PAWPAW MONTESPAN

4 green pawpaws, skinned and diced
thinly sliced ripe tomatoes
1 large Bermuda onion, sliced and fried
½ pound ground top round, browned
grated cheese

Cook pawpaws until tender. Mash and put a layer into greased baking dish. Cover with a thin layer of tomatoes, then meat and onion, then cheese. Repeat these layers until all ingredients used. Finish with pawpaw, sprinkle with cheese. Cover with bread crumbs. Bake at 350° F. for 40 minutes.

Another interesting plant that makes a good fence covering and can be used in a variety of ways is the CHRISTOPHINE, a member of the gourd family. As it is rather difficult to peel, it can be cut in quarters or left whole and dropped into boiling water for five to ten minutes. The skin is then easily removed. Christophines have a very delicate flavour and are delicious boiled until tender and served with melted butter or simmered in cream. They go very well with fish. Here are some other ideas.

CHRISTOPHINES STUFFED WITH MUSHROOMS

4 christophines (½ per person)
4 tablespoons butter
10 large mushrooms, chopped
3 shallots, chopped
5 tablespoons cream

Cut christophines in half lengthwise and drop into boiling, salted water. Drain after 10 minutes, peel and seed. Scoop out some of the flesh to enlarge the hollow. Melt butter in a skillet that has a close fitting lid. Cook the christophines slowly, covered until tender (about 30 minutes). In another skillet cook chopped mushrooms, parsley and shallots in butter. When juices are evaporated add cream. Arrange the christophines in a buttered baking dish. Fill the cavities with the mushroom mixture and sprinkle with fresh bread crumbs and dabs of butter. Bake at 350° F until browned. Grated Swiss cheese may be substituted for bread crumbs. Or the stuffed christophines may be covered with cheese sauce and run under a broiler until browned and bubbling.

FENNEL grows wild along roadsides and in open fields and is considered a nuisance by many. Actually it is a most interesting plant and has a variety of uses. An excellent fish sauce can be made with it, it can be cooked as a green vegetable and the young stalks peeled and eaten as celery. A pleasant cool drink can be made by steeping the flowers in boiling water. The seeds can be used as a flavouring in cakes, breads and cookies. Normally difficult to digest foods are made digestible when served with a fennel sauce. The cultivated variety is easily grown and makes an interesting addition to home vegetable gardens.

The SURINAM CHERRY came to Bermuda by way of Grenada. And it is another of our plants that is not only ornamental but has an interesting fruit. These are eaten ripe ... they are favourites of children to pick on the way home from school ... cooked or preserved.

SURINAM CHERRY JAM

Surinam cherries
Sugar

Wash and stone cherries. Measure fruit, to every cup of fruit you will need a cup of sugar. Sprinkle the sugar in layers between the fruit. Cover the bowl with a cloth and let stand overnight. Pour into a pot and bring to a boil, stirring. Simmer until the jam thickens. Pour immediately into sterilized jars and seal.

SURINAM CHERRY WALNUT BREAD

¼ pound margarine
1 cup sugar
2 cups sifted flour
3 teaspoons baking powder
1 teaspoon cherry extract (or vanilla)
2 eggs
½ cup Surinam cherries (or loquats pitted and peeled,
¼ cup chopped walnuts

Wash and pit cherries and press them in a strainer to extract most of the juice. In a mixing bowl blend soft margarine and sugar. When well blended add one cup of flour and one egg mixing thoroughly. Add the second cup of flour and second egg, again mixing thoroughly. Add baking powder and cherry extract and when thoroughly blended, stir in cherries and walnuts. Bake in a 9x5x3 inch loaf pan in a 350° F oven for approximately one hour or until cake tester comes out clean. Allow to cool in pan for about one hour, remove and place on cooling rack. Bread will slice easier on the second day.

FLAMING SURINAM CHERRIES

Into a chafing dish put butter, melt. Add pitted Surinam cherries and sugar. Cook to dissolve sugar. Add white rum. Serve flaming over vanilla ice cream.

The LOQUAT was introduced by Governor Reid about 1850. A native of Japan it came to Bermuda from Malta and grows well here. It has a yellow plum-like fruit that can be flavourful when ripe. A delicious liqueur is made from it. It is also made into tarts and a variety of jams.

LOQUAT JAM

6 cups loquats, measured after preparing
1 ounce green ginger, peeled and grated
4 cups sugar
1 cup water

Wash and stone fruit, save seeds and tie in a muslin bag. Put fruit, seeds and water in a pot, cook until tender. Add sugar and ginger. Remove bag of seeds. Boil until mixture sets. Bottle in sterile jars and seal.

LOQUAT CHUTNEY

1½ pounds seeded loquats
1 pound onions, chopped
½ pound grated apple
1 pound sugar
2 teaspoons mustard
2 teaspoons salt
1 teaspoon curry
1 tablespoon molasses
¼ teaspoon ginger
1 pint vinegar
2 cups water
¼ cup raisins

Wash, stone and cup up loquats into small pieces. Prepare apples and onions. Put all ingredients in pot and boil gently until soft and a good colour. Pour into hot jars and seal.

LOQUAT LIQUEUR

Prick 2 quarts loquats with a fork. Put in a jar with a tight top. Add 2 pounds rock candy and 1½ bottles gin. Shake every day for one month, strain and bottle.

A variation on loquat liqueur is this late 19th century version furnished by Mrs C. Vail Zuill.

MISS EDITH WILKINSON'S LOQUAT LIQUEUR

1 bottle brandy
1 ½ pounds loquats
¾ pound sugar
¼ teaspoon allspice
¼ teaspoon cinnamon

¼ teaspoon nutmeg
¼ teaspoon cloves
½ pint milk

Mince loquats and put with some seeds in air tight bottle, mix sugar with them, and let stand for a day. (The sugar will draw juice out of fruit). Add brandy and let stand for five weeks. Put into double flannel bag, let drain out that will, then squeeze the bag to get all the juice. Add spices and boiling milk to this liquor, and strain until clear through a double flannel bag. (The juice and rind of one lemon may be substituted for the spices. Steep the rind and add the juice when brandy is added to fruit).

These are by no means all of the old and favourite Bermudian receipts. Turn the pages to find more ... some old, some new ... and all favourites.

Bermuda's vegetation has been described by divers authors. Henry May who was shipwrecked here on the French ship of Captain de la Barbotière in 1593 called Bermuda a "terrestrial paradise". Captain John Smith in his *History of Virginia* wrote that the "prouidences and paines, haue offered diuers seeds and plants, which the soile hath greedily imbraced and cherished, so that at this present 1623 there are great abundance of ... whatsoeuer else may be expected for the satisfaction either of curiosity, necessity or delight". Then Governor Sir John Henry Lefroy, governor of Bermuda 1871-77, says in his two immense volumes, *The Memorials of the Discovery and Early Settlement of the Bermudas or Somers Islands 1515-1687 compiled from the Colonial Records and other Original Sources*, "that there are perhaps few places of such limited area which offer a greater variety to the intelligent visitor, or so much to gratify a botanical observer". And we who reside here in the 20th century strive to live up to our heritage and keep Bermuda a happy place to work and live for it is truly an island paradise.

Sources

Benjamin, S.G.W., *The Atlantic Islands as Resorts of Health and Pleasure*
Burland, Barbara, *Medicinal Plants and Old Time Remedies of Bermuda*
Lefroy, Lieut-General Sir J.H., *Memorials of the Bermudas 1515-1687* (2 volumes)
McCallan, E.A., *Life on Old St David's, Bermuda*
Smith, Louisa Hutchings, *Bermuda's Oldest Inhabitants*
Tucker, Terry, *Bermuda's Story*
Verrill, A.E., *The Bermuda Islands*
Wright, Louis B., *A Voyage to Virginia in 1609*
Zuill, Kitty, *A Bermuda Kettle of Fish*
Zuill, Mrs W.E.S., and Mrs Charles Burland, *Old Bermuda Recipes*

Chefs' Choices
Receipts from Bermudian Restaurants

Castle Harbour

The luxurious Castle Harbour Hotel, situated on its splendidly land-scaped 263 acre garden estate overlooking Castle Harbour, provides a beautiful setting for vacationers. "Sing-along" in The Isle O'Devils pub. Choose your favourite dishes at the Golf Club's Sunday Brunch. The Windsor Dining Room may justifiably take pride in its extensive Table d'Hôte and A la Carte menus and wine list. Here the gourmet will feel very much at home.

BAKED MARINATED FILLETS OF ROCKFISH

4 Rockfish (1½ pounds each)
12 tablespoons oil
juice of 4 lemons
5 grains saffron
½ teaspoon pepper
2 tablespoons chopped chives
salt
2 medium sized onions
4 tomatoes
2 tablespoons chopped dill, thyme and bay leaves

Clean and fillet the fish, wash and dry. Mix the oil with the lemon juice, saffron, pepper, chopped chives and salt. Marinate the fish fillets in this mixture for at least 6 hours. Wipe a casserole or baking pan with buttered paper. Peel and slice the onions and tomatoes and place on bottom. Remove fillets from the marinade and place in the pan. Sprinkle with chopped herbs. Bake in a hot oven (400° F) for 30 minutes.
  Serve with potatoes and salad.

CHICKEN CUTLETS "POZHERSKY"

2 pounds chicken breasts
1 cup milk
1 cup heavy cream
4 ounces white bread
4 tablespoons butter
salt and pepper
4 tablespoons breadcrumbs

Separate the meat from the bones and mince. Soak the bread in the milk and cream. Press out some of the excess moisture, add to the minced chicken and put through the mincer together. Add a tablespoon of melted butter, season with salt and pepper. Mix well and shape into cutlets. Cover with breadcrumbs and fry in hot butter on both sides until golden brown (this should take about 5 minutes), then cover with a lid and leave on a low heat for another 5 minutes. Serve with brown sauce or melted butter poured over the cutlets. Garnish with peas, green beans or rice.

Elbow Beach Surf Club

Bermuda's famous oceanside hotel enjoys a unique spot in the middle of this holiday island. Come up from the coral sand beach for a rum swizzle and lunch on the Surf Club Terrace Restaurant. In the evening relax over epicurean delights ... prime beef from the States ... New Zealand lamb ... lobster and rockfish from Bermuda's waters. Superior service and continental specialities await you at Elbow Beach!

POTAGE GERMINY (Sorrel Soup)
[serves 6]

½ pound fresh sorrel
2 tablespoons butter
5 egg yolks
1 cup heavy cream
5 cups beef consommé

Wash sorrel, remove hard stalks and cut in shreds. Melt butter in a saucepan, add the sorrel and cook until wilted and dry. Heat the consommé and pour over the sorrel. Mix the egg yolks with the cream. Pour the consommé and sorrel slowly over the cream mixture, stirring constantly. Return to stove and cook slowly, stirring with a wooden spoon, until the soup starts to thicken. (Do not let it come to a boil). Remove from heat, check seasoning. Pour into serving bowls. (Sorrel is a green, leafy vegetable, similar to spinach, but more acid. It grows well in Bermuda).

POULET AU VINAIGRE (Chicken with Vinegar Sauce)
[serves 4]

2 broiling chickens (2 pounds each)
6 ounces (12 tablespoons) butter
16 ounces (2 cups) good wine vinegar
8 ounces chopped shallots
1 teaspoon chopped parsley
salt and pepper

Cut the broilers into fourths removing back bones and wing tips. Put the chicken pieces into a shallow pan with 4 tablespoons butter, season, cover and start cooking slowly on top of stove. Finish the cooking in a slow oven (300° F). When chicken is tender and golden brown remove from pan. Place on a serving platter and keep warm. Add the shallots to the pan juices and brown. Add vinegar and reduce it by two-thirds. Lower heat and swirl in remaining softened butter, a little at a time, to thicken sauce. Check seasoning. Add chopped parsley. Pour the sauce over the chicken and serve. Rice pilaff, noodles or boiled potatoes go well with this dish.

CREME CARAMEL (Caramel Custard)
[*serves 6-8*]

Prepare the mould:

Heat 1 cup sugar in a heavy skillet, stirring constantly, until sugar melts and turns a golden caramel colour. Pour into a 1 ½ quart mould and turn mould so that the caramel coats the sides and bottom.

Custard:

Bring 1 quart of milk mixed with ½ pound (¾ cup) sugar to a boil. Remove from heat and add a vanilla bean. Let the mixture steep, covered, for 20 minutes, then remove the vanilla bean. Beat together 3 eggs and 8 egg yolks. Pour the milk gradually over the eggs, whisking constantly. Pour the custard into the caramelized mould. Place the mould in a pan of hot water (water should come half way up on the mould). Bake in 325° F oven until a knife inserted into center of custard comes out clean, about 1 hour. Remove from the water and chill. Turn the chilled custard out onto a serving platter. The top and sides may be decorated with whipped cream and red glacé cherries.

The Harbourfront Club

On Front Street, overlooking busy Hamilton Harbour, is The Harbourfront Restaurant, modelled after the inside of an ocean liner. The atmosphere is clublike during the luncheon hours but transformed to intimate dining at night. Or one can sit on the balcony and watch a cruise ship pass by. This popular restaurant boasts continental chefs who bring some of their native specialities to the kitchen of The Harbourfront.

LASAGNA
[serves 8]

1 pound package lasagna noodles
2 carrots, chopped finely
2 onions, chopped finely
2 celery stalks, chopped finely
1½ pounds ground beef
½ cup red wine
tomato paste
4 ripe tomatoes, chopped coarsely
nutmeg, salt and pepper
2 cups Béchamel sauce
6 hard-boiled eggs, grated finely
2 cups Mozzarella cheese, slivered
2 cups Parmesan cheese, grated

Parboil lasagna noodles, drain and pat dry.

Cook the vegetables in a small amount of oil over low heat until onions are transparent and carrots and celery slightly crisp. Brown the beef, drain and add to vegetables. Add wine, enough tomato paste to bind, tomatoes and seasonings. Cook slowly for 1 hour.

To prepare lasagna, pour meat sauce in the bottom of a large deep baking dish. Add noodles, more meat sauce, eggs, Béchamel sauce, Mozzarella and Parmesan cheeses. Repeat to make two layers approximately 3 inches high. Cook at 300° F for at least 1 hour or until lasagna is very firm.

HARBOURFRONT TORTA
[serves 10]

Sponge Cake:

7 egg yolks
¼ pound (½ cup) sugar
¼ pound (1 cup) flour

Combine egg yolks and sugar in the top of a double boiler and cook over low heat, beating constantly with a whisk until firm and fluffy. Remove from heat. With a rubber spatula fold in the flour. Pour into a well-greased cake tin and bake at 300° F for 1 hour. Allow cake to cool thoroughly, then slice in half through the middle. Pour either Lemon-Orange Syrup or rum over cake to prevent dryness.

This sponge cake may be served with a variety of frostings.

Chocolate Fudge Frosting:

6 egg yolks
4 ounces (½ cup) sugar
4 ounces (1 cup) flour
½ teaspoon grated lemon rind
1 quart (4 cups) milk

Combine egg yolks, sugar and flour and mix well. Add lemon rind. Bring milk to a boil and remove from heat. Add milk slowly to flour mixture, while stirring.

Cook over low heat, stirring constantly, until it is the consistency of custard. Add 4 tablespoons grated chocolate or 3 tablespoons cocoa. Mix well.

Horizons
AND COTTAGES

Dining in a 17th century manor house ... afternoon tea in the English tradition ... sumptuous buffet suppers ... dancing to Calypso music ... Bermudian and continental specialities ... after-dinner brandy in the cozy old English pub ... strolling through the lovely Bermudian gardens ... this is Horizons, a favourite of both visitors and Bermudians.

QUICHE LORRAINE
[*serves 8*]

Pastry:

1 pound flour
½ pound butter (or lard)
1½ cups water
1 pinch salt

Mix flour and butter gently. Combine water and salt and blend well with flour and butter to make a soft pastry. Let pastry rest ½ hour before using. Roll pastry to ¼-inch thick and place in a buttered or oiled 9-inch pie pan. Fill with the following mixture.

Quiche:

3 medium onions, sliced
8 ounces bacon, sliced
3 eggs, slightly beaten
½ pink milk (1 cup)
4 ounces Swiss cheese, grated
1 pinch each of salt, pepper, paprika and nutmeg.

Sauté onions and bacon over heat for 15 minutes. Drain and cool. Crumble the bacon. Combine the remaining ingredients, add the onions and bacon and pour into the prepared pastry shell.
Bake at 350° F for 25 to 35 minutes. Serve hot.

VEAL SUSANNE
[*serves 6*]

2 medium onions, chopped
4 ounces mushrooms, chopped
1 tablespoon tomato paste
6 veal cutlets (5 ounces each)

salt and pepper
4 eggs
1 cup Parmesan cheese, grated

Sauté the chopped onions and mushrooms over low heat until lightly browned. Add the tomato paste and cook quickly. Flatten the veal cutlets. Spread the mushroom mixture over the cutlets. Fold the cutlets in half and season with salt and pepper. Sprinkle both sides with flour. Blend eggs and Parmesan cheese. Dip the cutlets into this mixture. Sauté the cutlets in butter over medium heat until golden brown, turning once. Serve with spaghetti, macaroni or rice.

The LOBSTER Pot

Popular with "locals" and visiting yachtsmen, The Lobster Pot is modelled after a fisherman's home. It is decorated with antique fishing paraphernalia, and of course, every conceivable type of lobster pot.

First class Bermudian food, served in a convivial, casual atmosphere, is the order of the day. Their specialities are lobster, both Bermudian and Maine, served in a variety of ways, and lots of fresh fish. For landlubbers, there is a good selection of meat dishes.

KING SHRIMP PROVENCALE
[*serves 12*]

Peel one pound large shrimp (8-10 per pound) and place in a fireproof baking dish. Chop 3 peeled tomatoes, 1 clove garlic, 1 celery stalk and ½ onion. Sprinkle the vegetables over the shrimp. Add freshly chopped herbs, salt, pepper and paprika. Top with fresh breadcrumbs and dot with butter. Bake in a 375° F oven for about 20 minutes.

COQUILLES ST. JACQUES
[*serves 1*]

6 ounces fresh sea scallops
¼ cup water
¼ cup dry white wine
1 teaspoon lemon juice
¼ teaspoon salt
1 tablespoon butter
1 tablespoon flour
3 mushrooms, sliced
1 tablespoon Parmesan cheese, grated
½ cup mashed potatoes
1 egg yolk, beaten
2 tablespoons Hollandaise sauce

Put the scallops, washed well, into a skillet. Add the water, wine, lemon juice and salt. Cover and simmer until tender, about 5 minutes. Drain and reserve the liquid. Melt the butter, add the flour and cook two minutes. Add the reserved liquid (about ½ cup), bring to a boil and cook five minutes. This sauce should be thin. Add the scallops, mushrooms and then the cheese. Pour into a shallow buttered casserole or scallop shell. Spread the rim with the potatoes, then brush with the egg yolk. Bake in a 350° F oven for 10 minutes. Top the scallop mixture with the Hollandaise sauce and brown under a preheated broiler. Serve at once. Multiply this recipe for the desired number of servings.

BANANA FRITTERS

Peel ripe bananas (cut in chunks if large), roll in flour, then dip in beer batter. Fry in deep fat until golden brown. Drain and roll in cinnamon-sugar. Serve at once. If desired, heat black rum, light it and pour flaming over the bananas when serving.

Beer Batter:

½ cup flour
salt, a pinch
1 tablespoon melted butter
1 egg, beaten
½ cup beer
1 egg white, stiffly beaten

Combine the flour and salt. Mix the egg and melted butter. Stir in the beer gradually. Pour this mixture over the flour and stir only until smooth. Leave the batter in a warm place for about an hour. Then fold in the egg white.

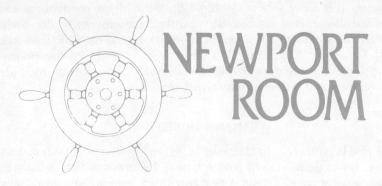

NEWPORT ROOM

The famous Newport to Bermuda Race is the theme for the Newport Room in the beautiful Southampton Princess Hotel. The service and food are reminiscent of the great old mansions of Newport. Boasting bone china, Waterford crystal and sterling silver, the unique splendor of this restaurant is surpassed only by its excellent food. For a memorable evening, dine in the Newport Room.

RICE VALENCIA
[*serves 4*]

3 cups cooked plain rice
4 ounces beef tenderloin
4 ounces chicken breast
2 scampi or shrimp
4 ounces whitemeat fish
1 green pepper
1 onion
2 peeled tomatoes
2 pimentos
olive oil
salt
1 teaspoon crushed peppercorns
thyme
2 cloves garlic, chopped
1 teaspoon curry
shredded coconut
chopped parsley

Cut the beef, chicken, scampi and fish into 1-inch slices. Cut green pepper, onion, tomatoes and pimentos into thin slices. Sauté vegetables in hot olive oil until almost tender. Do not overcook, they should be firm. Season with salt, peppercorns, curry, thyme and garlic.

Heat a heavy frying pan, add olive oil and sauté the beef, chicken, scampi and fish until brown. Season with salt and pepper. Add vegetables and rice. Mix well. Arrange mixture in a deep serving dish. Sprinkle with shredded coconut and chopped parsley. For attractive serving place serving dish on a platter with a banana leaf on it.

BERMUDA FISH PRINCESS
[*serves 4-6*]

1 rockfish (about 4 pounds)
olive oil
pinches of chopped garlic, oregano, dill
3 cups thickly creamed spinach
2 cups dry white wine (Chablis)
1 lemon
salt and freshly ground pepper

Butter Sauce:

10 ounces (1 ¼ cups) butter
2 teaspoons chopped parsley

Fillet the rockfish, leaving two nice fish fillets with no skin or bone. Place one fillet on a lightly oiled baking pan. Sprinkle on half the seasonings and cover with the spinach. Place the second fillet on top of the first, sprinkle over it the rest of the seasoning and a little oil, salt and pepper. Pour the wine around the fish and squeeze the juice of the lemon over it. Bake in a preheated oven (450° F) for 15 to 20 minutes. Remove to a heated platter and keep warm.

Butter Sauce:

Strain the juice from the baking pan into a small casserole. Bring to a boil and let it reduce until there are no more than 2 cups. Add softened butter and stir until it is melted. Add chopped parsley. Pass sauce separately. Serve with boiled potatoes and a green salad.

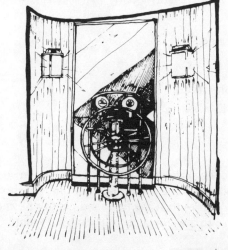

Rum Runners

In the heart of Hamilton is found this beautifully decorated restaurant of many atmospheres. The Garden Patio offers informal luncheons overlooking quaint Chancery Lane. The Load O'Mischief Pub featuring continental and Bermudian specialities is a favourite spot for lunch or dinner. Or sip your favourite cocktail on the iron grill balcony above Front Street.

FILLETS OF FISH "MEUNIERE"

Soak boneless and skinless fish fillets in milk for 30 minutes. Roll in seasoned flour and fry in butter until golden brown. Remove fillets to a heated serving platter and keep warm. Pour off fat from skillet and add fresh butter. Heat until light brown and pour over the fillets. Garnish with chopped parsley and lemon wedges. Serve with boiled new potatoes.

BABAS AU RHUM
[*serves 6*]

¼ cup milk, scalded
¼ cup butter
1 package yeast
¼ cup luke warm water
2 egg yolks
¼ cup sugar
1 egg
1¾ cups flour

Add the butter to the scalded milk. Cool. Dissolve the yeast in the water. Beat the egg yolks with the sugar, then beat in the whole egg. Add the milk and yeast mixtures then the flour and beat until smooth. Cover the batter and let rise in a warm spot (80° to 85° F) until doubled in bulk (about 1 hour). Punch down. Grease baba moulds and fill ⅔ full with the batter. Let rise, uncovered, until the batter rises a bit above the top of moulds (about 30 minutes). Bake in a 350° F oven until well browned (about 20 minutes). Remove from moulds and cool. Soak the babas in a light sugar syrup combined with rum. (If the babas are cold use a hot syrup, if warm use a warm syrup). Drain well and glaze with melted apricot preserves.

Pour over a bit more rum just before serving.

WATERLOT INN

For a very special occasion Waterlot Inn is the place to go. Situated in a Bermudian garden setting, it overlooks beautiful Riddell's Bay. Sail in to their private dock for brunch, dine leisurely on the terrace or by candlelight in one of the interesting rooms of this old Bermudian home. Whether for brunch, lunch or dinner, come to Waterlot Inn where good food and wines have become a tradition.

COQUILLE DE CRABE CHAMPENOISE
[serves 1]

3 ounces crabmeat
2 shallots, chopped finely
salt and pepper
½ ounce brandy
½ ounce dry white wine
1 tablespoon fish velouté
2 tablespoons heavy cream
3 tablespoons Hollandaise sauce

Toss the shallots in butter. Add crabmeat, salt and pepper. Moisten with brandy and wine. Cover and cook for 5 minutes. Add hot fish velouté and cream. Cover and cook for 5 minutes more. Pour into a small silver shell. Cover with Hollandaise sauce and glaze under the broiler. Garnish with a fleuron (puff pastry decoration) and a pinch of chopped parsley. Multiply recipe for desired portions.

Fish Velouté:

Make a white roux (melt 2 tablespoons butter, then add 2 tablespoons flour, blend to a paste and cook 2 minutes without colouring). Add 1 cup warm fish stock and stir quickly with a whisk until smooth. Add salt, pepper and white mushroom peelings. Cook, stirring occasionally, for about 45 minutes. Strain and stir until cold.

Fish Stock or Fumet:

Combine fish head and trimmings, minced onions, parsley stalks, mushroom parings, a celery stalk, bay leaf, lemon juice, salt and whole peppercorns. Cover with white wine and water (about 2 quarts). Cook for about 45 minutes and strain.

ESCALOPES DE VEAU A LA FRANÇAISE

Cutlets of veal may be cut from the loin of veal. Their weight varies from 2½ to 3 ounces. Allow 2 per person. Pound each cutlet lightly until very thin. Season with salt and pepper. Dredge in flour, then dip in whole eggs beaten with Parmesan cheese, salt, pepper and nutmeg. Sauté in very hot clarified butter. Each cutlet should be golden brown on both sides.

Arrange on a heated serving platter. Cover with Lemon Butter Sauce blended with a little *demi-glace* sauce. Garnish with a lemon basket and chopped parsley.

Lemon Butter Sauce:

Reduce dry white wine with lemon juice, then add soft butter and blend well with a whisk. *Do not let boil*. Add salt, pepper and a little *demi-glace* or veal juice. Keep warm.

Veal Juice:

Place broken veal bones with chopped carrots, celery and onions in a shallow baking pan. Brown in a very hot oven. Transfer them to a saucepan and cover with water. Add bay leaves, thyme, salt, peppercorns and fresh tomatoes

Cook slowly for 3 hours and strain. (Demi-glace is a very concentrated veal juice).

For informal dining overlooking the beach, there is the popular Whaler Inn. The food is excellent and after dinner there is dancing under the stars. As part of the large Southampton Princess complex, The Whaler Inn offers the usual standard of excellence in a casual, oceanfront atmosphere.

VEAL CUTLET EN PAPILLOTE
[*serves 1*]

1 6-ounce veal cutlet, trimmed
½ cup fresh mushrooms, sliced
1 tablespoon Bermuda onion, chopped
1 slice bacon, diced
1 tomato, peeled, seeded and chopped
¼ cup heavy cream
1 dash dry Vermouth or sherry

Sauté the veal cutlet in butter and remove from skillet. Dilute the cooking juices with Vermouth and cream and cook down. Fry the onion, bacon, mushrooms and tomato. Combine with the cream mixture. Season with salt, pepper, oregano and parsley. Cook over medium high heat for two minutes.

Spread out a sheet of aluminium paper cut in a heart shape. Oil well. Spread half the garniture in the middle of half the heart. Top with the cutlet and then the remainder of the garniture. Fold over the other half of the heart to enclose the cutlet. Pleat the edges to seal. Put the sealed heart on a baking sheet and bake in a hot oven (450° F) for about 15 minutes to puff out the heart. Serve at once. The heart is to be opened at the table.

BAKED BERMUDA FISH
[*serves 4*]

1 6-pound fresh Bermuda fish (snapper, rockfish, etc.)

Slit the fish lengthwise along the belly side. Completely separate the fillets from the bones. Cut the spine at both ends and carefully remove it.

Season the inside of fish with salt, pepper, lemon juice and Worcestershire sauce.

Stuffing:

4 shallots, minced
3 ounces bacon, diced
6 ounces spinach, chopped
4 bread rolls, cubed
1 cup cream or milk
2 eggs, beaten
2 ounces sliced almonds or walnuts
salt, pepper
chopped herbs: basil, sage, parsley, chives
1 cup dry white wine

Sauté the shallots with the bacon. Add the spinach and cook until wilted. Moisten the rolls with the cream and eggs. Add to spinach mixture. Season. Add herbs and nuts. Fill the fish with this mixture to give it a rounded appearance. Close by drawing the fillets together. Lay the fish on a well buttered deep oval dish, the size of which should be in proportion with the fish. Pour over the wine. Bake slowly (325° F) for about 45 minutes, basting often with the wine. When fish is a rich golden colour, cover with aluminium foil and finish cooking.

Serve on a silver dish decorated with parsley and lemon wedges. Garnish with boiled potatoes. Serve the pan juices separately.

Notes

Rock-Happy Receipts
Menus from Members of
the Bermuda Junior Service League

Breakfast and Brunch

Bermuda Christmas Breakfast

Fresh Citrus Salad
Croissants
Cassava Pie*
Orange Blossoms
(champagne and orange juice)

CASSAVA PIE FOR THE ENTIRE WEST FAMILY

As an American married to a Bermudian whose Christmas is not complete without Cassava Pie, the thought of attempting such a feat was staggering. Most cook books advise one to add a little bit of this and a pinch of that, pluck a couple of chickens and grate a few pounds of cassava. The older Bermudian cooks are not much more help. Recipes are extremely diverse, as are tastes.

This Christmas, I decided to attempt a Cassava pie. As a guideline I used several recipes gathered from Bermudians and my husband. The end result was a moist, semi-sweet, semi-savory Cassava Pie. It cuts beautifully and maintains its shape even when fried in butter. The most surprising part was that it is just as easy as making an apple pie.

6 pounds cassava
14 eggs
2½ cups butter (softened)
1 cup sugar
salt, fresh ground pepper, nutmeg, powdered cloves, allspice
4 pounds chicken breasts and thighs
(I have omitted pork as it has a tendency to spoil)

Boil chicken in a large pot with every kind of seasoning you have available. A couple of chopped carrots and stalks of celery will make the broth rich and savory.

Debone chicken and reserve broth.

Mix unfrozen cassava (that has been drained of its juices as much as possible) eggs and soft butter. Don't try mixing it with anything but your hands. Add sugar and a good pinch of all the spices and mix well.

In a large, well greased roasting pan put in about 1½ inches of the cassava mixture. Add the chicken in an evenly distributed layer. Top with remaining cassava (another 1½ inches) and prick with a fork. Then add about a cup of chicken broth and put it in the oven at 350° F. This will require approximately two hours of cooking. Remember to baste with chicken broth every ½ hour. The pie is done when a knife inserted in the middle comes out clean. Serves 12 or more.

This pie freezes beautifully and will allow you to enjoy it at Easter.

Jane West

Mrs Stephen West

Favourite Breakfast

Half Grapefruit
Sausages and Cheese
Johnny Bread*
Coffee

JOHNNY BREAD

This old Bermuda favourite comes in handy when my family wants something different on the breakfast scene.

1¾ cups flour
1 teaspoon baking powder
½ teaspoon salt
3 tablespoons vegetable oil
⅓ cup sugar
1 egg, slightly beaten
¼ cup milk
1 8-inch heavy frying pan

Sift flour, baking powder and salt in medium bowl. Add sugar. Add oil and egg and mix well with fork. Add milk gradually, continuing to mix with fork. Batter should be stiff but moist. Place on floured board and knead gently into ball. Roll out in circle to size of pan. Place in *hot* frying pan. Cook over medium to low flame until brown on both sides (approximately 7½ minutes each side). Serve hot with lots of butter.

Marilynn Simmons

Mrs R.D. Simmons

Sunday Breakfast "Annondale Farm", Maryland, U.S.A.

Freshly Squeezed Orange Juice
Choice of Dry Cereal and Cream
Cream Chipped Beef on Toast*

CREAM CHIPPED BEEF
(SERVES 4)

¼ cup minced onion
2 tablespoons minced green pepper
¼ cup salad oil
3 tablespoons flour
2 cups milk
¼ pound dried beef, shredded
1 teaspoon bottled thick meat sauce
¼ pound mushrooms sautéed and sliced (optional)

Brown onions and green pepper in salad oil. Blend in flour over low heat. Add milk gradually while stirring. When above mixture is smooth and thickened, add rest of ingredients. Serve hot over toast points or toasted English Muffins.

[*This creamed chipped beef is a weekly ritual at our house in the States.*]

Barbara Floyd

Mrs Richard Floyd

2 a.m. .... January 1st

Pea Soup*
John's Formula #380*
(rum punch)

PEA SOUP

If eaten in the first few hours of the New Year you will have good luck for the rest of the year.

1 large pot, filled with boiling water
1 package split peas (unsoaked)
1 large ham hock

2-3 bay leaves
carrots, onions, potatoes, celery
Tabasco
sherry

Cook until the peas have dissolved. Add the vegetables (coarsely chopped) and cook until tender. Add Tabasco and sherry to taste.

JOHN'S FORMULA #380

13 ounces Barbados Rum
3 ounces Gosling's Black Rum
2 ounces Bacardi Light Rum
1 tablespoon grenadine
1 tablespoon white Falernum
4 tablespoon lemon juice
13 ounces Dole's pineapple juice, unsweetened
13 ounces Trinidad grapefruit juice, unsweetened

Stir together in large pitcher. Serve over ice.

"yum, like drinking candy!"

Mrs John Trimingham

Traditional Bermuda Sunday Brunch

(for four)

Bloody Marys or Tomato Juice
Codfish with Egg Sauce*
Bananas, Boiled Potatoes
Toast with Marmalade

CODFISH WITH EGG SAUCE

1 pound boneless white salt cod
Worcestershire sauce
olive oil
4 bananas
small pickled pearl onions
4 medium-sized potatoes, boiled

EGG SAUCE

¼ pound butter
2 hardboiled eggs
⅛ teaspoon dry mustard
sherry

Wash codfish thoroughly, then soak overnight in cold water. Drain, cover with water and bring to boil. Simmer until tender.

Prepare sauce by melting butter in saucepan and adding chopped eggs, dry mustard and sherry to taste. Drain fish and serve on individual plates. Flake fish and add Worcestershire and olive oil as desired. Cover with egg sauce and complete dish with a peeled banana, pickled onions and potatoes. Buttered toast and marmalade add to flavour.

Serve with coffee.

Mrs Rendell Arton

Sunday Patio Brunch
(for eight)

Celery with Cream Cheese
Cocktail Sausages wrapped in Bacon
French Meatball Casserole*
Broccoli Spears
Bermuda onions, Avocado and Lettuce Salad
Red Burgundy
Crème de Menthe Parfait*

FRENCH MEATBALL CASSEROLE

4 tablespoons butter
1 cup chopped onion
1 clove garlic, minced
½ cup dry bread crumbs
2 pounds ground beef
2 eggs beaten
2 teaspoons salt
½ teaspoon freshly ground pepper
½ teaspoon thyme
2 tablespoons vegetable oil
1 pound mushrooms, sliced
1 10 ½ ounce can cream of mushroom soup
2 cups dry white wine

Melt 2 tablespoons butter in a skillet; sauté the onion 10 minutes. Mix in the garlic and bread crumbs; sauté 2 minutes. Remove from heat, and add the beef, eggs, salt, pepper, and thyme. Mix well. Shape into 2-inch balls.

Heat the oil and remaining butter in a skillet; brown the meatballs in it. Transfer to a casserole or baking dish. Sauté the mushrooms in the fat remaining in the skillet for 3 minutes. Add to the casserole. Mix the soup and wine; pour over the meat balls. (May be prepared ahead of time up to this point).

Cover casserole; bake in a 350° F oven for 45 minutes, removing the cover for the last 10 minutes. Taste for seasoning.

CREME DE MENTHE PARFAIT

[*My own concoction!!*]

In a large mixing bowl, beat 2 eggs white until stiff. Beat in 2 tablespoons sugar. Set egg whites aside. Into blender container put:
2 envelopes plain gelatin
½ cup green crème de menthe
½ cup hot milk

Cover and blend on high speed for about 40 seconds.
Add:
¼ cup sugar
2 egg yolks

Cover and blend for about 5 seconds. Remove cover and pour in:
1 jar Avoset Whipping Cream or 1 cup whipping cream

With motor on, immediately add:
1 heaping cup cracked or crushed ice

Blend for about 20 seconds, pour mixture over egg whites, and fold gently until mixed.

Pour into champagne glasses. Refrigerate.

At serving time, decorate with whipped cream and an 'After 8' or a similar chocolate mint.

Mrs Clive Pool

Luncheon

Lunch for the Ladies
(serves six)

Stuffed Tomatoes*
Empanadas de Horno*
(baked meat-filled pasties)
Saint Emilion
Watermelon

STUFFED TOMATOES

One tomato per person. Cut off top and hollow out tomato. Fill with a mixture of the tomato pulp and add 1 small tin of tuna fish, corn, chopped onion and season with pepper, salt, vinegar and oil. Serve in a bed of lettuce and decorate with mayonnaise.

EMPANADAS DE HORNO

Filling:
1 small onion, finely chopped
2½ teaspoons olive oil
6 tablespoons water
½ pound boneless, lean, tender beef cut into ¼ "cubes
5 teaspoons seedless raisins, soaked in ¾ cup boiling water for 10 minutes and drained thoroughly
scant teaspoon cayenne pepper
scant ½ teaspoon paprika
¼ teaspoon ground cumin seeds
scant ½ teaspoon salt
freshly ground pepper

Pastry:
2 cups plain flour
scant teaspoon salt
²/₃ cup butter, cut into ¼ "cubes
4 tablespoons cold water
2 hardboiled eggs, each cut into 8 wedges lengthwise
6 stoned olives

First prepare the filling:
  Put the onions, olive oil and 6 tablespoons of water into a large frying pan and boil over a high heat until the water is completely evaporated.

Add the meat and cook, stirring constantly, until it is browned on all sides. Stir in the raisins, cayenne, paprika, cumin, salt and a few grindings of pepper. Put the filling aside.

Preheat the oven to 400°F. To make the dough, mix the flour, salt and butter in a large bowl. Rub the flour and butter together until they blend and look like fine breadcrumbs. Pour the water over the mixture all at once and gather the dough into a compact ball.

Roll the dough out on a lightly floured surface making a rough circle about ⅛" thick. As you roll, lift up the dough from time to time and sprinkle a light dusting of flour under it to prevent the dough from sticking. With a pastry cutter 5 inches in diameter or an empty can of similar size, cut out 5 inch circles. (Or using a plate or saucer 5 inches in diameter as a pattern, cut out the circles). Gather the scraps of dough together into a ball and roll out again. Cut out similar 5 inch circles.

Place about 1½ teaspoons of the meat filling in the centre of each circle, leaving at least ½ inch of dough exposed around it. Top the filling with one piece of egg and two pieces of olive, and moisten the exposed dough with water. Fold the empanada in half to form a crescent and press the edges firmly together. Arrange the finished empanada on an ungreased baking sheet. Bake 10 to 15 minutes at 400° F (until golden brown). Makes 12-14 pastries.

Patricia Marsh

Mrs Michael Marsh

Chilean Sunday Lunch
(serves 8-10)

Clery*
(white wine and peaches)
Anticuchos*
(skewered spiced ox heart with chilli sauce)
Rice
Salsa Cruda*
(uncooked spiced tomato sauce)
Mixed Salad
Fruits

CLERY

2 pints (4 cups) white wine
1 can (16 ounces) peach slices (with syrup)

Mix above ingredients and serve over ice as a cocktail.

ANTICUCHOS

4-5 pound ox heart, trimmed and cut into 1-inch cubes.
Marinade:
⅜ pint (¾ cup) red wine vinegar
2 ½ teaspoons finely chopped, seeded and de-ribbed fresh hot red chilli
3 teaspoons finely chopped garlic
1 ½ teaspoons ground cumin seeds
1 ½ teaspoons salt
Freshly ground black pepper

Mix together in a large bowl the vinegar, fresh chilli, garlic, cumin, salt and a few grindings of pepper. Add the cubes of ox heart. If the marinade does not cover the ox heart, add more vinegar. Refrigerate, covered, for 24 hours. Remove the ox heart from the marinade and set them both aside.

Sauce:
¼ pint dried "bontaka" chillies, or substitute crushed chilli pepper.
2 ½ teaspoons liquid annatto, Tabasco or sherry peppers
2 ½ teaspoons olive oil
1 teaspoon salt

Break the dried chillies in half and brush out the seeds. Place the chillies in a bowl, pour ¼ pint (½cup) of boiling water over them and let them soak for 30 minutes. Drain and mix with ¼ pint (½ cup) of the reserved marinade, the annatto, oil and salt in the jar of a blender and purée at high speed for 15 seconds. (If you have no blender, put the chillies through the food mill and stir them into the marinade with the annatto, oil and salt).

Light a layer of coals in a charcoal grill and let them burn until white ash appears on the surface. Thread the ox heart cubes on skewers and brush them with the sauce. Grill 3-inches from the heat for 3 to 4 minutes, turning the skewers frequently and basting once or twice with remaining sauce.

Serve with rice and the following tomato sauce.

SALSA CRUDA
(makes about 1½cups)

4 medium-sized tomatoes (about 1 pound)
4 tablespoons finely chopped onions
1 tablespoon coarsely chopped fresh coriander
1 scant teaspoon drained, rinsed, and finely chopped canned "serrano" chilli, or crushed chilli pepper
½ teaspoon salt
⅛ teaspoon freshly ground pepper
Pinch of sugar

Drop the tomatoes into a pan of boiling water and remove them after 15 seconds. Run cold water over them and the skin will come off easily.

Cut the stem out of each tomato, then cut them in half crosswise. Squeeze the halves gently to remove the seeds and juice, and chop them finely. Put the tomatoes, onions, coriander, chilli, salt, pepper and sugar into a large bowl and mix together gently but thoroughly with a wooden spoon. Taste for seasoning. If the sauce is not to be served immediately, cover and refrigerate.

Salsa Cruda is traditionally served with cooked meats, poultry and fish.

Maisol P de Jones

Mrs Nicholas Jones

Never Fail Ladies' Luncheon
(serves four)

Betsey Outerbridge's Onion Soup*
Cheese Soufflé*
Tossed Green Salad
Rolls
Raspberry Cream*

BETSEY OUTERBRIDGE'S ONION SOUP

Sauté one pound of onions in margarine (because it's cheaper than butter, but if you're feeling affluent, live it up). When onions are limp, add two tins consommé, 1 teaspoon sugar, salt, pepper, Lawry's Seasoned Salt, and a large slug of sherry (and I mean, glug, glug, glug, glug). Simmer for about 15 minutes. Just before serving, put into individual ramekins, placing a fairly thick slice of French bread on top, covered with a slice of Swiss cheese. Put under broiler, and when Swiss cheese has melted, serve. And pass the Parmesan please!!!!!

CHEESE SOUFFLE

I like this recipe as it's an absolutely no-fail item which I throw together in the blender.

Into the blender put:
1 cup diced rat cheese, or cheddar (4 ounces)
2 tablespoons butter or margarine
4 tablespoons flour
1 teaspoon dry mustard

1 onion quartered
5 egg yolks
salt and pepper
1 cup hot milk

Blend on high speed until everything has been whirled down into the blades. Put into a saucepan and heat until it's thickened, but not gluey. In the meantime take those five egg whites and beat them until they are stiff. Pour the whites into the saucepan with the egg mixture and fold in with a rubber spatula. Pour into a soufflé dish (I just use a clear Pyrex one) and bake at 375° F for half an hour. This will serve six ladies that you don't know too well, but only about four close friends. And if anyone has any handy hints on how to clean the darn soufflé dish after you're finished, please let me know!

RASPBERRY CREAM

I hate to give this recipe because of all the folks who have had it at our house and insist it has been made with fresh raspberries (and who am I to correct them?).

This is also made in the blender, though I imagine you could do it with only a hand beater.

Into the blender put:
1 small package of raspberry Jello
½ cup boiling water

Blend on high speed for about 15 seconds, and then add:
¾ cup crushed ice (I usually throw in six to eight ice cubes, depending on their size).

When ice is blended in, and with machine still on, pour in:
1 cup heavy cream.

When cream is all poured in, turn off blender. Pour mixture into individual ramekins...if it's for a dinner party, (just one bowl if you're doing it for family) and chill until serving time, and I usually throw on a cookie just to brighten up the plate.

Joan Skinner

Mrs David Skinner

❉❉❉❉❉❉ ❉❉❉

Molasses mixed with water is stimulating.

❉❉❉❉❉❉❉❉❉

Sunday Luncheon

For Six

Honeyed Grapefruit*
Stuffed Fish Fillets*
California Rice Casserole*
Tomato & Cucumber Salad*
Asparagus
Seeded Hard Rolls
Angel Pie*

HONEYED GRAPEFRUIT

3 grapefruit
⅜ cup honey
6 strawberries

Cut grapefruit into halves, remove seeds. Cut around each section with a knife. Remove the core, and replace with 1 tablespoon honey plus 1 strawberry in each half. Chill until serving time. Serves 6.

STUFFED FISH FILLETS

2 to 2 ½ pounds fish fillets
1 cup sliced mushrooms
1 cup diced celery
½ cup chopped onion
2 cups croutons
1 teaspoon salt
⅓ cup butter
pepper to season
lemon juice

Brush fillets with melted butter and lemon juice. Sauté mushrooms, celery and onion in butter until just tender, not soft. Combine with croutons, salt and pepper to taste. Spread the fillets with stuffing and roll up like a jelly roll. Secure with tooth picks. Place fillets in buttered oven baking dish and cover with the following sauce.

Sauce:
½ cup dairy sour cream
½ cup catsup
½ cup mayonnaise
½ cup white wine

Blend all above ingredients in blender. Bake uncovered in 375° F oven for 30 minutes. Serves 6.

This dish can be prepared ahead. Leave the sauce until the end and make sure fish are not too cold before baking.

CALIFORNIA RICE CASSEROLE

1 pound pork sausage, cut in bite size pieces
2 cups converted rice, uncooked
1 large green pepper, diced
2 large onions, chopped
10 stalks celery, chopped
½ teaspoon salt
pepper to taste
3 envelopes dry Lipton Noodle Soup
9 cups water
½ pound blanched almonds (optional)

Brown sausage. Add rice to sausage and brown thoroughly, stirring constantly. Add green pepper, onion, celery, salt and pepper.

In a separate pot, cook the Lipton Noodle Soup in 9 cups water. Add to the rice mixture and let stand 1 hour. Add almonds and stir. Bake at 350° F for one hour.

This recipe serves 10 to 12. The casserole can be made the day before and reheated. For half the amount, cook in two casseroles and freeze one. Reheat one casserole after thawing when needed.

ANGEL PIE

[Make this Pie the day before]

Meringue shell

Filling:
2 tablespoons all-purpose flour
1 cup sugar
⅛ teaspoon salt
¼ cup water
¼ cup lemon juice
4 beaten egg yolks
¼ teaspoon almond extract
2 cups whipping cream

Mix flour, sugar and salt. Add water and lemon juice, stir until smooth. Add 4 beaten egg yolks and mix well. Cook over low heat until mixture is thick, stirring constantly. Remove from range, add almond extract. Chill. Whip 2 cups cream until stiff. Fold half of the whipped cream into the filling. Pour into meringue shell. Top with remainder of whipped cream. Let stand 24 hours in refrigerator before serving.

Mrs Michael Robinson

Luncheon Menu for Four

Chicken Curry Soup*
Quiche Lorraine*
Tossed Salad
French Bread
Frozen Lemon Meringue*

CHICKEN CURRY SOUP

½ cup milk
1 can cream of chicken soup, undiluted
1 teaspoon curry powder
1 cup crushed ice
½ cup heavy cream

Put milk, soup and curry powder in electric blender. Cover and run on low speed until mixed. Add ice and cream. Cover and run on high speed until completely smooth. Serve cold; garnish with chopped chives and thin cucumber slices.

QUICHE LORRAINE

8 ounces Swiss cheese
9-inch unbaked pie shell
6 slices bacon, crisply cooked
2 cups half milk, half cream
4 eggs
1 tablespoon cornstarch
½ teaspoon salt
¼ teaspoon grated nutmeg
dash of cayenne pepper
2 tablespoons grated Parmesan cheese

Grate Swiss cheese and put in pie shell. Crumble bacon and mix cheese and bacon evenly. Whip milk and cream mixture, eggs, salt, cornstarch, nutmeg and cayenne. Pour over cheese and bacon. Sprinkle Parmesan cheese on top. Bake at 375° F for 40 minutes. Let stand 10 minutes before serving.

FROZEN LEMON MERINGUE

3 egg yolks
½ cup of sugar
juice and grated rind of 1 lemon
3 egg whites
½ pint heavy cream, whipped
Vanilla wafer crumbs

Beat yolks in top of double boiler. Add sugar and juice and rind of the lemon. Cook until thick, stirring to keep smooth. Cool and add stiffly beaten egg whites, and whipped cream. Butter a 1½ quart loaf pan, line with wafer crumbs, pour in meringue, then sprinkle top lightly with a few crumbs. Cover and freeze. Leftover meringue keeps well in freezer.

Sally Gregg

Mrs Arthur Gregg

Committee Luncheon for Six

Papaya and Lime Juice
Chicken Salad
Bibb Lettuce and Walnuts
Gougère*
Alsatian Riesling
Fresh Strawberries

GOUGÈRE

1 cup water
6 tablespoons butter
1 teaspoon salt
⅛ teaspoon pepper
1 cup sifted flour
4 eggs
1 cup diced Comté cheese (or Swiss cheese)

This is a cream puff type dough incorporating Comté cheese and baked in a crown shape.

Combine water, butter, salt and pepper in a saucepan and heat until butter melts and mixture boils. Add the flour, all at once, and stir until mixture leaves sides of the pan and forms a ball. Beat in the eggs one at a time. Reserve two tablespoons of cheese, stir rest into mixture. Place heaping tablespoons of dough on a lightly greased baking sheet in a crown shape, about 10 inches in diameter, leaving hole in center. Sprinkle dough with reserved cheese. (The gougère may be frozen at this moment and while still frozen placed in a 425° F oven for 45 minutes). Cook at 425° F about 45 minutes, should be well puffed and browned. If not sufficiently cooked it will collapse. Serve warm.

Margaret de Marcy

Mrs Hubert de Marcy

August Luncheon

Fresh Fruit Salad with Cottage Cheese
Honey-Sesame Dressing*
Hot Yeast Rolls
Favourite Chocolate Cake with Orange Icing*
Iced Tea

HONEY-SESAME DRESSING
(makes 1 cup)

⅔ cup mayonnaise
⅓ cup honey
¼ cup sesame seeds

Brown sesame seeds in a little oil in skillet. Drain on paper towel. Mix honey and mayonnaise well and add browned sesame seeds.

Combine your favourite fresh fruits and arrange on lettuce cups with scoop of cottage cheese. Pass Honey-Sesame dressing.

FAVOURITE CHOCOLATE CAKE

Compliments of Kay Smith

4 ounces unsweetened chocolate
1 cup boiling water
2 cups sugar
¼ cup butter or margarine
.2 cups flour
1½ teaspoons baking powder
¼ teaspoon salt
½ cup sour milk
2 eggs
1 teaspoon vanilla

Preheat oven to 325° F.
  Melt chocolate in double boiler and add boiling water. Stir well. Cream butter and sugar in large mixing bowl and add chocolate to it. Sift flour, baking powder and salt in separate bowl and add alternately to wet ingredients with sour milk. Beat eggs until fluffy and add to above with vanilla. The batter will be thin. Pour into a greased 9 x 12 inch sheet cake pan. Bake for 50 minutes, or until toothpick comes out clean. When cake springs back, cool on wire rack and frost. Cut into squares to serve. The remainder can be frozen successfully.

ORANGE ICING

3 tablespoons butter
3 tablespoons frozen orange juice concentrate
2 cups icing sugar

Melt the butter in medium saucepan. Add orange juice. Add the icing sugar gradually using electric mixer. If too thick add a bit more orange juice.

Maria Smith

Mrs Edward Smith

Winter Luncheon
(Serves 6)

Bloody Marys
Sausage and Mushroom Pie*
Sliced Tomatoes
Bermuda Oranges with Rum

SAUSAGE AND MUSHROOM PIE

Pastry:

Combine 1½ cups flour, 6 tablespoons butter (cut into pieces), 2 tablespoons vegetable shortening and ¼ teaspoon salt. Blend until combined and add 3 tablespoons ice water. Form into ball, knead a few seconds and chill for 1 hour. Roll the dough out and line 9 inch pie shell or 6 individual tart shells. Line with wax paper, fill with rice and bake 10 minutes at 400° F. Remove rice and bake 8-10 minutes more.

Sauté 1 pound of sliced mushrooms in ¼ pound butter until brown. Add ½ pound cooked sausage cut into pieces. Stir in 1 cup heavy cream and simmer 5 minutes. Make a *beurre manié* of 1 tablespoon soft butter and 1 tablespoon flour mixed together. Add to simmering cream mixture in bits, stirring. Add 1 tablespoon lemon juice, salt and pepper. Simmer 5 minutes. Spoon into shell and reheat in oven. Sprinkle with chives.

Sally Cooper

Mrs Alex Cooper

Favourite Luncheon for Four

Tomato Soup*
Cheese Soufflé*
Cold Sliced Ham
Peas
Tossed Salad
Loquat and Apple Crisp*

TOMATO SOUP

1 can tomato soup
1 can consommé

Heat the soups and add sherry to taste. Garnish with sour cream or chopped parsley just before serving.

CHEESE SOUFFLE

2 tablespoons butter
4 tablespoons flour
2 cups milk
8 eggs, separated
1 ½ cups grated cheese (or more)
pinch of salt
pinch of seasoning salt

Melt butter, add flour, then gradually add milk. Stir until smooth and thick. Beat in egg yolks, one at a time. Add cheese and seasonings. Let cool at least an hour, then add well beaten egg whites. Pour into buttered soufflé dish. Bake for ½ hour at 350° F.

LOQUAT AND APPLE CRISP

Stew skinned loquats with plenty of sugar
Stew 2 peeled apples.
Take 2 ½ cups stewed loquats and add stewed apples.
Add: ½ teaspoon nutmeg, 1 tablespoon cinnamon, ¼ teaspoon salt and sugar to taste. (Preserved ginger can also be added).
Put with 10-inch round flan pan. Cover with the following topping.

Topping:
¾ cup flour
1 cup sugar
⅓ cup butter
½ teaspoon salt

Rub above together and put over fruit. Bake at 350° F for about 40 minutes. Serve with lemon sauce or vanilla ice cream.

Ruth M. Burrows

Mrs Alex Burrows

Cold Chilean Luncheon
(serves 6)

Pisco Sour*
Sopa de Aguacate
(avocado cream soup)
Fruta de Mar*
(cold seafood with corn and rice salad)
Assorted Pastries
Cheeses

PISCO SOUR

2 pints Peruvian brandy (or French brandy)
½ pint lemon juice
sugar to taste

Mix all ingredients and serve in cocktail glasses over ice.

FRUTA DE MAR

Seafood

2 or 3 small live lobsters, boiled, cut in half, cooled and shelled;
    or 3 pounds live crabs, boiled, cooled and shelled;
    or 3 pounds prawns, boiled, shelled and cooled;
    or a combination of lobster, crab and prawns

To assemble, stir the corn mixture into the cooled rice and heap in a mound in the center of a large serving dish. Arrange the cold seafood attractively on or around the rice, and serve the sauce separately in a small bowl.

Corn and Rice salad:

6 ounces (approximately 1 cup) fresh corn kernels, cut from 2 ears of corn or 6 ounces defrosted frozen corn kernels
2 medium-sized tomatoes, peeled, seeded and coarsely chopped or ¼ pint (½ cup) canned plum tomatoes, drained and chopped

2 ½ tablespoons white wine vinegar
5 teaspoons olive oil
2 ½ teaspoons coarsely chopped fresh coriander
¼ teaspoon finely chopped, seeded fresh hot chilli
½ teaspoon salt
Freshly ground black pepper
4 cups cooked rice, cooled

Bring 3 cups of water to the boil over a high heat in a small saucepan. Drop in the corn kernels, return to the boil and cook uncovered for 3 minutes, stirring frequently. Drain the corn thoroughly and return it to the saucepan. Stir in the tomatoes, vinegar, olive oil, coriander, chili, salt and a few grindings of pepper; leave the mixture at room temperature for 1 hour.

Sauce:
1 whole egg (or 2 egg yolks)
¾ cup olive oil
3 tablespoons lemon juice
1 teaspoon tomato paste
½ teaspoon finely chopped, seeded, fresh hot chilli
½ teaspoon dry mustard
½ teaspoon salt
¼ teaspoon white pepper

Drop the whole egg into the jar and blend at high speed until the egg is thick and creamy. Without stopping the machine, remove the cover and gradually pour in the olive oil in a slow stream. When the sauce is very thick, add the lemon juice, tomato paste, fresh chilli, mustard, salt and white pepper, and blend for 5 seconds.

To assemble, stir the corn mixture into the cooled rice and heap in a mound in the center of a large serving dish. Arrange the cold seafood attractively on or around the rice, and serve the sauce separately in a small bowl.

Mairol P de Joues

Mrs Nicholas Jones

❖❖❖❖❖❖❖❖❖❖

Whale meat gives vigour to sickly children.

❖❖❖❖❖❖❖❖❖❖

Tea

After-School Snack

"Glug" or Lemon Concentrate*
Ginger Snaps*
Orange Coffee Cake*

GLUG

6 grapefruit
3 lemons
Oranges, if desired (I don't)
2 - 2 ½ pounds sugar (4-4 ½ cups)
2 pints boiling water (4 cups)
1 ounce citric acid

Squeeze the juice from all the fruit and grate some of the rind. Mix all the ingredients and let stand overnight. Strain and then store in glass jars or milk cartons if freezing. This makes about 3 quarts.

Add 1-2 ounces of the concentrate to a juice glass and fill with water and ice.

Very refreshing and a great way to use up the fruit.

LEMON OR LIME CONCENTRATE

2 ½ cups sugar
2 cups boiling water
1 ounce citric acid
½ cup lime juice

Mix all the above ingredients together and store in a large glass jar which is airtight. This will keep for several weeks in the refrigerator or can be put into cleaned milk cartons and frozen for several months.

With limes, you may wish to add a bit more sugar and with sweet lemons, less sugar - this will depend on whether you like it tart or sweet. It will yield about a quart and a half.

Excellent added to ice tea. When mixing it by the glass, add about 1 ½ to 2 ounces of the concentrate to a small juice glass and add water.

"Glug" or this concentrate may be used to make popsicles.

GINGER SNAPS

¾ cup oil (or melted shortening)
1 scant cup white sugar
1 egg
4 tablespoons molasses
2 cups flour
1 teaspoon salt
2 teaspoons baking soda
1 teaspoon cinnamon
½ teaspoon cloves

Add sugar to oil and cream well. Add beaten egg and molasses, mix well. Add dry ingredients last. Drop by teaspoon and flatten with a fork.
  Bake 350° F for 10-15 minutes.
  Let cool before moving from sheet.

And if the mothers come too, serve this quick and easy Orange Coffee Cake.

ORANGE COFFEE CAKE

1 egg
8 tablespoons melted shortening (or oil)
½ cup milk
grated rind 1 orange
½ cup sugar
½ teaspoon salt
4 teaspoons baking powder
2 cups flour
½ cup orange juice

Add beaten egg to ½ cup of sugar. Stir in the shortening or oil and rind. Blend salt, baking powder and flour together and add to the above alternately with the milk. (This mixture will be quite thick). Add the orange juice and put into a 8-inch cake pan which has been greased and dusted with a tablespoon of flour.

Topping:
2 tablespoons soft butter or margarine
½ cup brown sugar
1 teaspoon nutmeg
1 teaspoon cinnamon

Mix all these together and sprinkle over the top of the batter.
  Bake 375° F. for 30 to 35 minutes.

Neil Kempe

Mrs Richard Kempe

English Supper for Four

Bunty's Senegalese Soup*
Sausages with Onions*
Mashed Potatoes
Buttered Peas
Custard and Stewed Fruit

BUNTY'S SENEGALESE SOUP

1 cup fresh cream
1 tin cream of celery or chicken soup
chives
1 cup cracked ice
1 teaspoon curry powder

Put everything into blender for 30 seconds or until frothy. Add chives. Keep in refrigerator until serving time.

SAUSAGES WITH ONIONS

10 ounces milk
2 onions
8 large pork sausages

Slice or chop onions. Boil in water until tender. Drain. Lay sausages on the onions. Season. Pour on milk and bring to boil. Simmer for ¼ hour. Remove sausages to warm serving dish. Mix 1 heaping tablespoon flour in small amount of cold milk and add to sauce pan. Bring to boil again for one minute or until sauce thickens. Pour over sausages.

Bunty Macdonald-Smith

Mrs A. MacDonald-Smith

❊❊ ❊❊❊❊❊❊ ❊❊

Place Red Sage [lantana] leaves in cupboards to keep moths away.

❊❊❊❊❊ ❊❊❊❊❊

Polly's Party Menu

(from Polly Smith, age 10)

Assorted Sandwiches
Sugar Drop Cookies*
Bermuda Glass Candy*
Party Punch*

SUGAR DROP COOKIES

$^2/_3$ cup shortening
1 egg
$^3/_4$ cup sugar
1 teaspoon vanilla
1 $^1/_2$ cups flour
1 $^1/_2$ teaspoons baking powder
$^1/_4$ teaspoon salt
$^1/_2$ cup broken nuts
4 teaspoons milk
$^1/_2$ cup raisins

Set oven at 375° F. Put a bit of shortening on waxed paper. Rub it over the cookie sheet until lightly greased.

In a bowl, soften shortening with a wooden spoon. Mix sugar in thoroughly. Add egg. Beat until fluffy and unstreaked. Add vanilla and mix well.

Sift flour. Sift again with baking powder and salt. Set aside until needed.

Add milk to shortening-egg mixture. Add flour mixture, nuts and raisins. Drop by teaspoons on sheet, bake about 12 minutes. Remove and sprinkle with sugar.

BERMUDA GLASS CANDY

3 cups sugar
$^1/_2$ cup water
1 teaspoon vinegar
1 teaspoon butter
food coloring
pinch of salt
flavoring

Put sugar, water and vinegar in a pot over low heat, stirring until sugar is dissolved. Boil gently without stirring for 20 minutes. Add butter and salt. Continue cooking for ten minutes or until crack stage is reached (290° on candy thermometer).

Remove from stove, stir in desired food colouring and flavouring without scraping the sides of the pot.

Pour about ⅛ inch thick into 20 muffin tins that have been well greased with shortening, not butter. When cool, turn pans upside down on table and tap out. Wrap individually in plastic wrap.

PARTY PUNCH

1 large tin pear nectar
1 large can frozen orange juice
2 teaspoons strawberry essence
juice of four lemons or limes
3 quarts of water
1 cup sugar or to taste
red food coloring

Mix all ingredients, adding a few drops of red food coloring. Serve well chilled over ice.

Maria Smith

Mrs Edward Smith
(Polly's mother)

German Kaffeeklatsch

Kruemeltoertchen*
(crumb tarts)
Apfelkuchen*
(apple cake)
Nusstorte*
(nut layer cake)
Sandtorte*
(very fine pound cake)
Weisse Maeuse*
(white mice)
Coffee with whipped cream

In Germany, "Tea-time" consists of a cup of filter coffee served with milk, sugar and a little whipped cream on top. With it you serve delicious cakes and pastries.

KRUEMELTOERTCHEN (crumb tarts)

½ pound (1 cup) butter
½ pound (1 cup) sugar
1 egg
1 pound (4 cups) flour

Mix all ingredients together to make a soft dough. Fill bottom and sides of muffin tins with dough. Fill with your favourite jam (not too much) and sprinkle some dough on top of jam. Bake at 350° F for about ½ hour or until golden brown. Makes about 24 tarts.

APFELKUCHEN (apple cake)

½ pound (2 cups) flour
¼ pound (½ cup) butter
⅛ pound (¼ cup) sugar
1 egg
Pinch of salt
1 teaspoon baking powder
5 large apples

Mix together all ingredients to make a soft dough and line a 10-inch or 11-inch spring form and sides with it. Prepare 5 large apples, cut into small pieces and boil with very little water, some sugar and lemon peel for about 10 minutes. Drain and cool. Spread onto the dough and top with some crumbs made of:

¼ pound (1 cup) flour
¼ pound (½ cup) butter
⅛ pound (¼ cup) sugar
pinch of salt

Bake at 350° F for 45 - 60 minutes or until top is slightly browned.

NUSSTORTE (nut layer cake)

½ pound (2 cups) walnuts (ground)
1 cup sugar
12 egg yolks
8 egg whites
¼ teaspoon salt

Beat 12 egg yolks, add sugar and beat, add nuts and beat. Whip egg whites with the salt until very stiff. Fold egg whites into nut mixture. Pour into four 9 to 10-inch cake pans and bake at 325° F for about 25 minutes. (Butter pans well or line with buttered wax paper). Remove and cool layers and fill with following cream filling:

3 cups of heavy cream, beaten stiff
3 tablespoons Hershey's chocolate syrup
2 teaspoons instant coffee
3 tablespoons liqueur (Tia Maria or Grand Marnier)

Before spreading filling on first layer, spread some jam mixed with a little Rum on it, then put cream on top. Also spread on sides of cake and chill very well before serving. Can also be made in advance and frozen. Needs 3 - 4 hours to defrost.

SANDTORTE (very fine pound cake)

3 whole eggs
2 egg yolks
½ pound (1 cup) butter
½ pound (1 cup) sugar
lemon peel of one lemon
1 teaspoon vanilla
½ pound (1¼ cups) cornstarch
2 tablespoons flour
2 tablespoons Rum
2 egg whites

Cream the butter well. Add 3 whole eggs and 2 egg yolks and beat very well. Add sugar, lemon peel and vanilla and rum creaming well after each addition. Slowly fold cornstarch and flour into the mixture. Beat egg whites stiff and fold into the mixture carefully. Pour into a loaf-type pan, (well greased) and bake at 350° F for 60 - 75 minutes, until lightly browned on top. Let cool in oven before removing from pan.

WEISSE MAEUSE (white mice)

1 cup walnuts, finely chopped
½ cup brown sugar
1 cup butter
2 cups flour

Mix all ingredients together to make a soft dough. Shape into 2 inch long crescents and bake on greased cookie sheet at 350° F until golden brown, about 30 minutes. Makes about 30 mice.

Amelie's Scheland

Mrs Dieter Scheland

Dinner and Supper

Christmas Dinner in Bermuda

This is a family affair and so the job of preparing the great feast is usually distributed among the female members of our family. The following menu is made up of family recipes.

Stuffed Roast Turkey
Giblet Gravy
Baked Ham
Mashed Potatoes
Fresh Carrots
Fresh Green Beans
Cassava Pie*
Cranberry Sauce*
Christmas Pudding and Hard Sauce*

CASSAVA PIE

We usually make this several days before.

12 pounds grated cassava
2 pounds sugar
1 tin condensed milk
2 ¼ dozen eggs, unbeaten
2 pounds butter, melted
3 tablespoons salt
2 teaspoons nutmeg
Brandy to taste
5 pounds chicken
2 ½ pounds cubed pork

Put cassava into large bowl. Cover with sugar. Add next 6 ingredients in order of appearance. Blend thoroughly. Place half of this mixture in large greased baking pan or use several small ones, making sure that there is at least 1 ½ inches of batter in each.

Put chicken and pork in a pot, cover with water and add salt and pepper to taste. Bring to a boil and simmer till meat is just tender. Remove the chicken meat from the bones then ladle meats over the cassava batter adding a little stock. Cover the meat filling with the rest of the cassava leaving a small hole in the centre to baste through.

Bake at 350° F for 1 hour. Reduce heat to 250° F and bake another 3 hours. Baste hourly by pouring stock through the hole in crust. Cool in pan and then cover with a damp cloth, this keeps the crust soft. To serve, slice and warm in the oven or in butter in a frying pan. Serves 50.

Cassava pie is eaten all during the Christmas holidays. It freezes so well that some families even keep it for Easter.

CRANBERRY SAUCE

If you ever get your hands on some fresh cranberries here is a simple recipe for a sauce.

To one quart of cranberries add 1 pound of sugar and 1 pint of water. Cook slowly, without stirring in order to preserve the fruit whole, for 10 - 15 minutes. Pour into jars and seal.

CHRISTMAS PUDDING

1 pound sugar
1 pound butter
1 dozen eggs, separated
1 pound bread crumbs (grated and sifted)
vanilla
1 pound dark raisins
½ pound light raisins
1 pound candied fruit
½ pound candied cherries
½ pound dates (optional)
Brandy

Soak fruit in rum or brandy overnight.

Cream together butter and sugar till light, beat in egg yolks. Beat egg whites till stiff and fold into creamed mixture. Add the sifted bread crumbs and then gradually add the fruit, which should be floured lightly first. Add vanilla and brandy to taste. Put into well greased pudding molds (2 or 3), cover each with a damp floured cloth and foil, then with top of mold. Boil in a covered stew kettle with water ¾ up the mold (add water as it evaporates) for 2 hours or till done. Remove immediately from kettle.

This recipe is very rich and will serve approximately 25.

These puddings are usually made a month to two months before Christmas and frozen or stored in their molds.

When the time comes to serve, warm the pudding by steaming it in its mold in a kettle of water then invert onto a serving dish. Pour heated brandy over it and set alight, bring flaming to the table and serve with Hard Sauce.

HARD SAUCE

½ cup butter
2 cups sifted icing sugar
3 tablespoons brandy

Cream butter till fluffy. Add the sugar and brandy alternately and beat well till smooth. Chill in serving dish.

Mrdy Williams
Mrs Chet Williams

❋

Any-Night-of-the-Week Dinner for Four

Bermuda Fish with Island Sauce*
Rice
Grilled Tomatoes
Buttered Green Peas
Nannas Brownies*

BERMUDA FISH WITH ISLAND SAUCE

2 pounds firm white Bermuda fish fillets
(Silk or grey snapper is especially good)
1 tablespoon butter or margarine
1 tablespoon flour
1 cup milk
½ teaspoon salt
½ teaspoon freshly ground pepper
1 tablespoon curry powder
1 ounce diced crystallized ginger
2 firm Bermuda bananas, peeled and sliced
1 tablespoon sugar
juice of ½ lemon or lime

Dip fish fillets in flour and pan fry until tender. In the meantime, make sauce in medium size saucepan. Melt butter, add flour and blend. Add milk gradually, mixing with fork. Add next seven ingredients and cook over low heat until slightly thickened. Serve over fish fillets.

86

NANNA'S BROWNIES

These brownies are compliments of my mother-in-law, Kay Smith, who always keeps a batch in the freezer for visiting grandchildren. They are the moistest, chewiest brownies I have ever tasted.

2 ounces unsweetened chocolate
¼ pound butter or margarine
2 eggs
1 cup sugar
½ cup flour, sifted
¼ teaspoon baking powder
¾ cup chopped walnuts
1 teaspoon vanilla
pinch of salt

Melt butter and chocolate in small saucepan over low heat. Beat eggs in medium sized mixing bowl and then add sugar. Beat again until light and fluffy. Add sifted flour, baking powder and salt gradually. Add butter and chocolate and beat again. Stir in nuts and vanilla. Spread in 9 inch square buttered pan and bake 30 minutes at 350° F. Cut in squares when cool. May be frosted with chocolate icing.

Maria Smith

Mrs Edward Smith

Dining at "Surrey Hill"

(Serves 8)

Steven's Pâté Maison*
Veal à la Surrey Hill*
Rice - Green Beans
Hot Rolls
Brolio Rosé
Charlotte Russe*
Coffee

My favourite recipes are those which can be prepared long in advance. Steven's Pâté Maison therefore is special.

STEVEN'S PATE MAISON
(Make three days before required)

Marinate: 16 ounces frozen chicken livers for 2 hours
in
2 tablespoons Madeira wine
2 tablespoons white wine
2 tablespoons finely chopped onion
1 dried, crushed Bermuda spice tree leaf
or
1 commercial bay leaf

Place in Blender:
1 slice bread
6 Walls pork sausages, skins removed
the livers and the marinade

Mix thoroughly. Line an oven proof dish with stretched bacon strips. Set in pan of hot water. Pour in liver mixture. Bake covered for 1¼ hours at 350° F. Refrigerate when cool. Serve with toast.

This is good with cocktails.

VEAL A LA SURREY HILL

5 pounds veal, cut in small pieces as for stewing
salt and pepper
3 tins cream of mushroom soup
4 onions, sliced
Tabasco
½ cup sherry
1 carton sour cream

The day before:

Brown veal well in butter. Place in large covered casserole. Sprinkle with salt and pepper. Spoon soup over the top. Fry onions and put on top.

Add ½ cup water and the Tabasco to the frying pan. Bring this to a boil, stirring in the browned bits. Pour over casserole. Cover and bake for 45 minutes. Add sherry and bake for another 30 minutes, uncovered. Cool and refrigerate covered.

Next day: Heat casserole until bubbly. Add sour cream and a bit more pepper. Stir and continue baking uncovered for 10 minutes.

Serve over rice.

CHARLOTTE RUSSE

[*Also made the day before*].

Dissolve ¾ tablespoon gelatin in ¼ cup cold water. Add this to a ⅓ cup of scalded milk.Beat in ⅓ cup of confectioners sugar. Cool. Flavour with 1½ tablespoons brandy. Fold in 1 cup of thick cream, whipped, and small bits of candied fruit - such as cherries (no pineapple).

Refrigerate in mold which has been lined with lady fingers. Unmold before serving.

Mrs Francis N. Trott

Bermuda Luau
(Serves 4)

Cream of Shrimp Soup*
Sweet and Sour Chicken*
Rice
Chinese Vegetable Bowl*
Chocolate Tea Balls*
or
Lemon Moments*
Tea

CREAM OF SHRIMP SOUP

To one tin of canned cream of shrimp soup, add one small can of chopped shrimp and a good dash of sherry.

SWEET AND SOUR CHICKEN

2½ pounds chicken, cut up
2 tablespoons oil
½ green pepper
1 clove garlic
1 large onion
Ginger, salt and pepper
2 rings pineapple
(save juice from can for sauce)

Sprinkle salt, pepper and ginger on chicken. Fry until brown on all sides in oil. Slice onion into rings and green pepper and pineapple into chunks, crush garlic clove. When chicken is brown add remaining ingredients and cook slowly until chicken is tender. Remove chicken to casserole and make sauce.

Sauce:
5 ounces pineapple juice
5 ounces chicken stock (use bouillon cube)
1 tablespoon tomato purée
2 tablespoons sugar
3 ounces vinegar
2 tablespoons cornstarch
Soy sauce, to taste

Boil pineapple juice, stock, tomato purée, sugar and vinegar together. Mix cornstarch with a tablespoon water and when stock mixture is boiling pour it in and stir till thickened. Add soy sauce.

Add sauce to vegetables in pan and simmer two or three minutes to mix flavours. Pour over chicken. This can be refrigerated and then reheated at 350° F for half an hour. (May be frozen). Serve with rice cooked in liquid drained from Chinese vegetables.

CHINESE VEGETABLE BOWL

1 large onion, sliced
2 cups sliced celery
1 6-ounce can mushrooms, sliced
1 package frozen Italian style green beans
1 can Chinese vegetables, (i.e. Chop Suey vegetables including bean sprouts, water chestnuts and bamboo shoots) drained.
Soy sauce

Lightly fry onion in a little oil till soft. Add celery and liquid from mushrooms. Cover and steam 5 minutes. Add beans and canned vegetables and steam covered 7 to 10 minutes or until beans are tender but still crisp. Sprinkle with salt and good tablespoon of soy sauce. Good hot or cold.

CHOCOLATE TEA BALLS

½ pound butter
½ cup confectioner's sugar
2 envelopes liquid chocolate for cooking
1 teaspoon vanilla
2 cups flour
¼ teaspoon salt
¾ cup finely chopped walnuts

Mix butter and sugar, add chocolate and beat well. Add vanilla, flour and salt. Mix till blended. Stir in walnuts. Roll into small balls, place on cookie sheet and bake 14 - 17 minutes at 400° F. While still warm shake in bag with confectioner's sugar to coat. Makes 65 cookies.

LEMON MOMENTS

½ cup butter
½ cup sugar
½ cup flour
¾ teaspoon baking powder
1 whole egg & 2 egg yolks

Grease well an 8" x 8" pan. Mix ingredients in order given and spread in pan. Bake until brown (about ½ hour) at 350° F. While cake is baking, mix 1 can condensed milk with the rind and juice of 2 lemons. Beat well for 5 minutes. Spread over cake layer.

Topping:

Beat 2 eggs whites with ½ cup sugar, ½ teaspoon lemon extract (or ½ teaspoon lemon juice). Spread over condensed milk layer and sprinkle with ¼ cup coconut. Bake at 400° F for 10 minutes or until brown. Cool and cut into squares.

Diana Diel

Mrs Coles Diel

Winter Dinner for Four

Spinach Soup*
Roast of Beef
Baked Suet Pudding*
Jacket Potatoes with Sour Cream and Chives
Beans and Broccoli*
Coffee Marshmallow Jelly*

SPINACH SOUP

A subtle flavour which even those who hate spinach will love!

1 large package frozen spinach
1 large onion, finely chopped
2 tablespoons butter
¼ cup plain flour
1½ cups chicken stock

pinch ground nutmeg
salt and pepper
¼ pint pouring cream

Cook spinach as directed on packet. Drain but reserve ½ cup of liquid. Melt butter in saucepan, add onion and fry lightly until soft. Stir in flour and cook slowly for 2 or 3 minutes. Remove pan from heat and gradually add stock, then return to heat and bring to the boil. Add nutmeg, spinach and spinach liquid and bring to boil again. Place all in the blender and purée. Adjust seasoning, boil again. Pour into heated serving dish, swirl in the cream and serve.

BAKED SUET PUDDING

A crisp and crunchy alternative to Yorkshire pudding, for serving with a roast of beef.

1 cup flour
¼ cup suet, grated
Little salt and pepper

Mix all together with a little cold water to form a firm dough.

Place in greased pie dish and bake at 425° F for ½ hour, until light golden brown.

The same mixture as above, dropped by spoonfuls into a stew about ¼ hour before serving time, produces delicious dumplings.

BEANS AND BROCCOLI PUREE

In blender, purée:
1 package frozen green beans, cooked
½ package chopped broccoli, cooked
A little melted butter
Salt and pepper

Heat and serve.

COFFEE MARSHMALLOW JELLY
WITH BANANAS

Place in a double boiler over boiling water:
1 pound marshmallows
Pour over them and stir until they are dissolved:
2 cups boiling coffee
Stir in 1 cup of chopped nuts.
Place all in wet ring mold and chill until firm.

Invert onto serving dish, fill center hole with sliced fresh bananas and top with whipped cream. Sprinkle chopped nuts around top of ring of jelly.

Pat Maher

❄

Dinner From Deutschland

(Serves 8)

Jansons Fretelse*
Königsberger Klopse*
(East Prussian meatballs)
Sauerkraut
Mashed Potatoes
Tossed Salad
Strawberry Sherbet*

JANSONS FRETELSE

15-20 anchovy fillets
6-8 medium potatoes
2-4 medium yellow onions, sliced
bread crumbs
Margarine or butter
1 cup light cream

Cut Potatoes as for French fries (chips).

Butter an oven-proof casserole. Put in one layer potatoes, one layer onions, one layer anchovies. Repeat.

Spread top with bread crumbs and brown at 400° F for 15 minutes. Remove from oven, pour cream all over and put back in oven. Bake about 45 minutes at 350° F.

Great with lots of beer!

KÖNIGSBERGER KLOPSE

4 slices bread
½ cup milk
2 pounds hamburger
4 ounces anchovy fillets, drained, chopped
3 eggs
1 small onion, grated
2 tablespoons grated lemon rind

salt and pepper
pinch nutmeg
2 envelopes instant beef broth or
  1 teaspoon granulated beef broth
4 cups water
¼ cup butter
¼ cup flour
1 teaspoon sugar
½ cup dry white wine
2 tablespoons well drained capers
1 tablespoon lemon juice

Place bread slices in milk, let stand until absorbed. Mash with fork. Combine hamburger, ½ the anchovies, all the eggs, onion, lemon rind, salt and pepper, nutmeg and bread, mixing lightly. Shape into 32 balls. Combine beef broth and water in large skillet. Boil. Add meatballs. Simmer uncovered 15 minutes or until no longer pink in centre. Remove with slotted spoon to a deep platter. Reserve cooking liquid. Make sauce: Melt butter or margarine, stir in flour and sugar. Cook until bubbly, stirring constantly. Gradually add wine and 2 cups of cooking liquid, continuing to stir until mixture has thickened and bubbles 1 minute. Stir in capers, lemon juice and remaining half of anchovies, stirring until anchovies are blended with sauce. Spoon over meatballs.

Serve with sauerkraut and mashed potatoes, mixed vegetables and/or tossed salad. Freezes very well.

STRAWBERRY SHERBET (4)

1 package frozen strawberries
Grand Marnier, Kirsch or orange Curaçao
Orange zest and juice

Defrost strawberries. Pour off juice. Put into blender and blend until pulp. Freeze in covered container. When semi-frozen, remove add 1 teaspoon - 1 tablespoon of any liqueur. Add peel of orange, finely chopped and about 1 tablespoon juice. Put into blender and blend thoroughly. Replace in freezer, covered.

  Peaches and apricots work well too. Avoid grapes, raspberries (unless puréed) or blueberries.

Mrs Michael Weiss

Dinner at "Skyline"

(Serves 8)

Poularde Portugaise*
Rice
Tossed Green Salad
Crusty Rolls
Rum Chiffon Pie*

POULARDE PORTUGAISE

5 pounds chicken breasts, boned and cut into bite size pieces
4 tablespoons flour
1½ teaspoon salt
¼ teaspoon ground pepper
2-3 tablespoons olive oil
3 tablespoons butter
1 large onion, sliced
1 clove garlic, minced
1-2 green peppers, seeded and cut into squares
1 cup button mushrooms
3 large tomatoes, cut into thick slices
¼ cup finely chopped parsley
1½ cups dry white wine or half wine and half chicken broth
½ cup pitted sliced green or black olives
½ cup heavy cream

Dust chicken pieces with mixture of flour, salt and pepper. Heat oil and butter in skillet, (electric skillet at 350° .F) brown chicken until crisp but not cooked through. Remove. Add onion and garlic, cook until soft. Add green pepper and mushrooms, cook about 2 minutes. Replace chicken over vegetables or pour vegetable mixture in casserole and place chicken over vegetables. Arrange tomato slices and parsley over top. Add wine, cover tightly and cook on low heat for 30 to 40 minutes or bake in oven set at 350° F for 45 minutes. Add olives and cream during last 10 minutes.

RUM CHIFFON PIE

1 baked 9-inch pie shell
1½ envelopes (1½ tablespoons) unflavoured gelatin
½ cup cold water
3 eggs, separated
½ cup sugar
1 cup strong black coffee
3 tablespoons dark rum
1 cup heavy cream, whipped

Soften gelatin in cold water. Beat egg yolks till thick, add sugar, beat again, add ¼ cup coffee. Cook in top of double boiler over hot water, stirring until mixture thickens (about 5 minutes). Add softened gelatin and remaining coffee. Chill until mixture starts to set. Beat with rotary beater until fluffy. Add rum. Fold into whipped cream and egg whites (stiffly beaten). Pour into baked pie shell and chill until firm.

Mary-Jane Pantry

Mrs Gary Pantry

Winter Sunday Night Supper

Bermuda Fish Chowder*
Sherry Peppers*
Whole Wheat Rolls*
Loquat Pie*

FISH CHOWDER

2 fish heads
2 fish fillets
  or 6 small heads
2 teaspoons salt
1 teaspoon thyme
3 bay leaves
3 spice leaves
1 teaspoon peppercorns
1 teaspoon ground cloves
4 tablespoons bacon fat
3 large onions, chopped
8 stalks celery, chopped
1 clove garlic, chopped
2 green peppers, chopped
1 pound 12-ounce tin tomatoes
10 ounce tin consommé
1 cup ketchup
8 sprigs parsley
2 tablespoons Worcestershire sauce
½ teaspoon curry powder
juice of 1 lemon
2 pounds potatoes
5 or 6 carrots
1 large pawpaw (green)
½ medium turnip
black rum and sherry to taste

Place fish heads and fillets in large kettle and cover with water, then add next 6 ingredients. Bring to a boil and cook till meat leaves the bones, about 15 minutes.

In large frying pan melt bacon fat and cook onions, celery, garlic and green peppers till soft. Add next 7 ingredients and simmer for 30 minutes. Peel and cut into bite size pieces potatoes, carrots, pawpaw and turnip. Par-boil in salted water.

Strain fish broth then remove fish from bones and return meat, broth and spice leaves to kettle (please, no bones). Now add vegetables and their stock and stir in contents of the frying pan. Salt to taste. Flavour with black rum and sherry to taste. Simmer gently for 3 ½ hours, stirring occasionally. About 20 servings. It freezes well. Let guests add drops of Sherry Peppers to taste.

SHERRY PEPPERS

This should be made ahead so that it may sit for several weeks in order to obtain that zing all Bermudians love.

It is very simple - just fill a jar or decanter half full with red bird peppers and fill up with sherry. Keep adding sherry as needed. Add several drops to fish chowder.

WHOLE WHEAT ROLLS

I make these by the dozens, freeze them and then use as required. Would you believe no-kneading and they rise in the refrigerator.

1 ½ cups white flour
1 package active dry yeast
1 ¼ cups skim milk
 (instant if you wish)
¼ cup brown sugar
¼ cup shortening
1 teaspoon salt
1 egg
2 - 2 ¼ cups whole wheat flour

Combine flour and yeast in large mixing bowl. In saucepan combine next 4 ingredients, heat till warm (110 - 120 degrees), stirring constantly.

Now pour into mixing bowl with the egg. Beat at low speed for half a minute, scrape the bowl then beat at high speed for 3 minutes. Then stir in the whole wheat flour, enough to make a soft dough. Cover with a damp cloth and put in the refrigerator for at least 3 hours (may be left for 3 days).

About 2 hours before serving shape dough into the shapes you wish, cover and let rise till double, about 1 hour. Bake at 400° F for 10 minutes. Makes 2 - 3 dozen.

LOQUAT PIE

I have discovered that when the loquats come into season, I can make pie filling, pour it into sterilized jars and seal it, and so make loquat pie all year round. Must be stored in cool dark place.

4 cups loquats
1 cup sugar
½ cup water
2 tablespoons flour
½ teaspoon cinnamon
⅛ teaspoon allspice
⅛ teaspoon salt
⅛ teaspoon ginger
pastry

Wash and quarter loquats, removing the seeds. Combine loquats and water and cook till tender, about 15 minutes. Sift dry ingredients together then stir into loquats.

Cook over medium heat till mixture thickens, remove from heat and cool. Prepare pastry for 8 or 9 inch pie plate. When loquat filling is partially cooled pour into pie dish containing bottom crust. Cover with top crust and bake at 450° F for 10 minutes then 350° F for 30 minutes.

Mary Williams

Mrs Chet Williams

"La Fête des Rois"
(Twelfth Night Dinner for Eight)

Champignons farcis*
(stuffed mushrooms)
Gigot d'agneau à la broche*
(spit-roasted leg of lamb)
Haricots verts au beurre
(buttered green beans)
Château Cheval Blanc, Saint-Emilion
Fromages de France
(French cheeses)
Les Musigny, Bourgogne
Galette des rois*
Château Guiraud, Sauternes [chilled]

Twelfth Night is celebrated in France by serving a special cake called "La Galette des Rois". Before baking, a bean or a small ceramic king is inserted into the pastry from the underside. At serving time the pastry is cut into as many pieces as there are guests. A child is asked to go under the dinner table and as the hostess points to a piece she asks the child to say for whom it is. The person finding the bean in his piece is crowned king and he chooses a queen (or vice-versa). During the rest of the evening whenever the king drinks the guests follow suit exclaiming, "le roi boit!" (the king's drinking). The windows of the pastry shops in France are filled with these cakes as Twelfth Night approaches. What fun it is to choose one and be given the golden crowns for the king and queen! We keep this tradition every year here in Bermuda.

CHAMPIGNONS FARCIS

16 fresh very large mushrooms
8 medium mushrooms
3 thin slices cured ham, chopped
3 tablespoons parsley, chopped
2 ½ cups béchamel sauce
1 egg yolk
salt, pepper, nutmeg
½ cup Swiss cheese, grated

Remove stems from large mushrooms. Melt one tablespoon butter in a skillet and sauté large mushroom caps, hollow side up, five minutes. Be careful not to break them. Remove from skillet and salt and pepper lightly. Chop the remaining mushrooms and stems; sauté until their liquid evaporates. (More butter may be needed in skillet). Remove from heat and add ham and parsley.

Make two and one-half cups béchamel sauce (medium thick white sauce). Add egg yolk and seasonings. Pour one cup of this sauce into the chopped mushrooms and ham along with a pinch of cheese. Taste for seasoning. Fill the mushroom caps with this mixture. Spread the remaining mixture in the bottom of a shallow baking-serving dish. Place filled mushroom caps on top. Pour remaining béchamel (thinned with milk if too thick) over all. Sprinkle with the cheese. This recipe may be made ahead to this point and covered with plastic wrap or foil for several hours. Bake (uncovered) in 375° F oven 15 to 20 minutes or until bubbling.

GIGOT A LA BROCHE

1 6-pound leg of lamb
2 cloves garlic, sliced
1 cup broth (lamb or beef)
watercress

Have butcher trim leg of lamb, removing tail and pelvic bones. Leave shank bone intact. (You can easily do this yourself). Save bones and trimmings and make a broth for the sauce. Cut small slits in the lamb and insert the garlic. Sprinkle with salt and pepper. Put on the spit of your rotisserie, securing well with the skewers. Place shallow pan underneath to catch the drippings. (If you have no rotisserie, put in roasting pan and baste occasionally). Sear lamb in a preheated 500° F oven for 10 to 15 minutes and then lower heat to 350° F. We usually cook a leg of lamb about one hour...it is rare. Cook longer if desired, but it should be pink. When done, remove to a heated platter and surround with watercress. Attach a carving handle or paper frill to shank bone. Deglaze the drippings with one cup of lamb broth (or use canned beef broth), scrapping to unstick all particles. Carve the leg of lamb at the table and serve on warmed plates. Pass the sauce separately.

GALETTE DES ROIS

1 pound puff pastry
1 egg, beaten

Roll the pastry into a circle one-eighth inch thick. Make a slit on the under side and insert a bean. Brush the top with beaten egg. With a point of a sharp knife cut a design of leaves on top. Slash around the outside edge of pastry at one-inch intervals. Prick top in several places. (This helps it to rise evenly). Bake in a preheated 450° F oven for ten minutes, then reduce heat to 350° F. Bake until pastry is golden and dry (about 15 minutes more). Serve at once, if possible, otherwise, keep in a dry place until serving time.

Margaret de Marcy

Mrs Hubert de Marcy

Relieve arthritis by applying chopped "Match-Me-If-You-Can" leaves soaked in vinegar to the affected areas.

Beware of plantanes in your garden: "one year's seeding, seven year's weeding"

Dinner At "The Chimneys"

(Serves 8)

Spicy Tomato Soup*
Crêpes Véronique*
Curly Endive Salad
dry white wine
Grasshopper Pie*

SPICY TOMATO SOUP

¼ cup onions, chopped
¼ cup carrots, chopped
2 tablespoons butter
parsley
4 cups tomato juice
white pepper
¼ teaspoon ground cloves
bay leaf
salt
⅛ teaspoon thyme
2 cups consommé

Sauté onions and carrots in butter. Add rest except consommé and simmer 1 hour. Strain, add consommé and heat again.

CRÊPES VÉRONIQUE

Crêpes:
¾ cup flour
1 tablespoon sugar
½ teaspoon salt
3 eggs
1 cup milk
1 tablespoon melted butter

Mix flour, sugar and salt.

Beat eggs until blended and sift flour mixture over eggs. Stir in milk and butter. Beat to a smooth batter.

Heat 8-inch frying pan and grease lightly.

Measure scant ⅓ cup batter into pan. Tilt pan so that the batter covers bottom evenly. Cook 1 to 2 minutes and turn.

Roll crepes, cover and keep warm. Repeat until all batter is used.

Filling:

3 whole chicken breasts
1 chicken broth cube
1 cup water
6 tablespoons butter
⅓ cup flour
1 cup cream
1 cup halved seedless grapes
½ cup sliced almonds

Simmer chicken breasts in water with broth cube till tender then remove bones and skin. Pour broth into measuring cup to make 1½ cups.

Melt butter, stir in flour and make sauce with broth and cream. Add chicken, grapes and almonds.

Spoon ⅓ cup chicken mixture into each crêpe and roll again. Place crêpes in single layer in baking dish. Spoon remaining mixture over crêpes.

Bake 350° F for 20 minutes.

GRASSHOPPER PIE

1 cup chocolate wafer crumbs
¼ cup sugar
2-3 tablespoons butter, melted

Combine and press into bottom of 9-inch pie pan and let cool.

Combine in top of double boiler:
¼ cup milk and ¾ pound miniature marshmallows. Stir until melted, then remove from heat and let cool, stirring frequently.

Combine ¼ cup green crème de menthe and 2 tablespoons white crème de menthe, add to marshmallow mixture.

Fold mixture into 3 cups whipped cream. Turn into crust and freeze overnight. Remove from freezer ½ hour before serving.

Sally Cooper

Mrs Alex Cooper

❧❧❧❧❧❧❧❧❧

Lemon juice keeps the hands beautifully soft and white.

❧❧❧❧❧❧❧❧❧

Dinner and Bridge

(serves 6)

Chicken Liver Dip*
Sour Cream Noodle Bake*
Baked Crusty Tomatoes*
Bibb Lettuce Salad
Orange Custard*

CHICKEN LIVER DIP

½ pound chicken livers
¾ teaspoon salt
½ teaspoon Tabasco
¼ teaspoon nutmeg
1 teaspoon dry mustard
1 tablespoon Cognac
¼ clove garlic
½ cup plus 1½ tablespoons butter

Throw everything in blender after chicken livers are cooked (pink) and put in small serving crock. Refrigerate.

SOUR CREAM NOODLE BAKE

Cook, rinse and drain 1 eight ounce package Egg Noodles
Melt in skillet: 2 tablespoons butter
Add: 1 pound Hamburger and cook until just off pink
Add: 1 (8 ounce) can tomato sauce
1 teaspoon salt
¼ teaspoon Garlic Salt
⅛ teaspoon pepper
Cover and simmer five minutes.
 Fold together: Noodles, 1 cup cottage cheese, 1 cup sour cream, 1 cup onions (green), chopped.
 Put half the mixture into bottom of 2½ quart casserole and cover with half meat mixture. Repeat again and sprinkle top with lots of coarsely shredded Cheddar cheese. Refrigerate or freeze. When ready to serve return to room temperature and bake at 350° F for 30-35 minutes or until cheese is bubbling.

BAKED CRUSTY TOMATOES ... Serves 12

½ cup butter
2¼ teaspoons seasoned salt
1½ teaspoons garlic powder

1½ tablespoons ground cumin
1½ cups cornflake crumbs

Spread all this on cut side of 12 tomatoes cut in half. Place in shallow dish and refrigerate overnight or for a few hours. Bake at 300° F for 30 minutes after letting tomatoes sit at room temperature for ten minutes.

ORANGE CUSTARD

1½ cups of sugar
5 eggs
3 egg yolks
Grated rind from two oranges
1½ cups fresh orange juice, strained
1 cup heavy cream

Place ¾ cup of sugar in a large heavy skillet over high heat and cook, stirring constantly with a wooden spatula, until sugar has caramelized. Pour immediately into a two quart casserole tipping dish back and forth until bottom is completely covered. Work quickly or the syrup will harden. Set aside to cool. Combine eggs and egg yolks with the remaining sugar and beat at high speed with electric mixer, until thick and creamy. Thoroughly stir in the orange rind, juice and heavy cream. Pour into cold prepared casserole and place in a large pan. Add enough hot water from the tap to reach about two-thirds the depth of the mold and bake in a preheated 325° F oven one hour or until a knife comes out clean. Refrigerate until cold and unmold before serving.

Mrs John P. Faiella

If you heat a lemon before squeezing, you will get nearly double the amount of juice.

Five Flag's Dinner
(Serves 6-8)

Shrimp à la King over Herb Biscuit Patties*
Baked Ham
Tomato Pilaf*
Candied Bermuda Sweet Potatoes*
Green Salad
Fruit Spanish Cream*

SHRIMP A LA KING

1 7-ounce package frozen shrimp
2 packages fillets of sole
¼ cup butter
½ cup celery, thinly sliced
2 tablespoons finely chopped onion
1 10-ounce can sliced mushrooms
⅓ cup flour
1 ¾ cups milk
½ teaspoon salt
½ cup shrimp cooking liquid
2 egg yolks, slightly beaten
¼ cup sliced stuffed olives

Cook frozen shrimp according to package directions, reserving ½ cup of the cooking liquid.

Bake fillets of sole at 350° F for 20 minutes. Cool, then separate into 1 ½ inch pieces. In top part of double boiler, cook celery, onion and mushrooms in melted butter until soft. Add flour, then milk, stirring constantly until mixture thickens. Combine shrimp cooking liquid, egg yolks and salt. Add some of the hot mixture to egg yolks, then blend into remaining hot mixture. Place over hot water and continue to stir until yolks are cooked, about 5 minutes. Gently stir in shrimp, fish and olives.

Serve over the following Herb Biscuit Patties.

HERB BISCUIT PATTIES

1 ¾ cups flour
4 teaspoons baking powder
½ teaspoon salt
1 tablespoon sugar
½ cup shortening (part butter)
⅔ cup milk
¼ cup chopped parsley

¼ teaspoon thyme
½ teaspoon marjoram

Combine dry ingredients and stir to blend. Cut in shortening. Add milk, stirring with a fork until all flour is moistened. Turn onto lightly floured board and knead gently for 20 seconds. Roll dough ½ inch thick and cut 12 2½-inch rounds. Using a small bottle cap (about 1½ in diameter) cut out circles in half of the rounds. Moisten edge of each whole round and place cut-out rounds on top. Bake at 450° F for 10-12 minutes.

TOMATO PILAF

2 28-ounce cans stewed tomatoes with onion, celery, and green pepper.
Worcestershire sauce
Pepper and salt
8 slices buttered toast (cool then cube)
8 strips bacon (fry, cool then crumble)
Parmesan cheese, grated

Season tomatoes to taste with Worcestershire sauce, pepper and salt.
   In greased baking dish layer tomatoes, cubed toast and crumbled bacon. Repeat, then top with cubed toast and crumbled bacon. Sprinkle with Parmesan cheese. Bake 350° F for 1 hour.

CANDIED BERMUDA SWEET POTATOES

8 medium sweet potatoes
⅓ cups water
1 cup firmly packed brown sugar
2 tablespoons butter

Wash potatoes and boil until tender. Drain, peel and cut in halves lengthwise. Bring water and sugar to a boil, dip potatoes into syrup and place in greased baking dish. Dot with butter and add remaining syrup. Bake in hot oven (400° F) 20 minutes basting occasionally with syrup.

FRUIT SPANISH CREAM

1 envelope plain gelatin
¼ cup cold water
1½ cups milk, scalded
3 eggs, separated
⅓ cup sugar
1 teaspoon vanilla
1 cup shredded canned pineapple, drained
1 cup raspberries
1 tablespoon lemon juice
½ cup macaroon crumbs

Soften gelatin in cold water 5 minutes, add milk. Combine egg yolks and sugar, add gelatin mixture and cook over hot water for 5 minutes stirring constantly until sugar is dissolved. Cool and chill until slightly thickened. Add vanilla, pineapple, raspberries, lemon juice and macaroon crumbs; fold in stiffly beaten egg whites. Turn into mold or parfait glasses and chill until firm.

Yields: 6 small portions.

Double above for 8 - 10 good portions. (Can be made day before serving)

This same menu can be used as a buffet by adding curry [to taste] to the shrimp dish and serving it over rice instead of the Herb Biscuit Patties and omitting the candied sweet potatoes.

Mrs Jimmy Amos

Winter Dinner At "Alton Hill"

(Serves Six)

Cream of Beet Soup*
Roast Leg of Lamb with Herbs*
Mint Apple Dressing*
Baked Winter Squash
Broccoli with Cream Cheese Sauce*
Green and White Parfait*
Coffee

CREAM OF BEET SOUP

2 tablespoons butter
2 tablespoons flour
1 teaspoon salt
¼ teaspoon pepper
4 ounces (¾ cup) strained beets (baby vegetables may be used)
4 cups milk
Chopped parsley

Melt butter, blend in flour, salt, pepper. Stir over medium heat until bubbly. Add strained beets, bring to the boil, stirring. Then add milk, check seasoning. Serve hot garnished with parsley.

ROAST LEG OF LAMB WITH HERBS

3-5 pound leg of lamb
1-2 teaspoons salt
½ teaspoon pepper
½ teaspoon garlic salt
1 teaspoon chopped basil leaves
1 teaspoon rosemary leaves, crushed

Preheat oven to 325° F. Place lamb in roasting pan, sprinkle with seasonings and herbs. Mix dressing and place in roasting pan with lamb. Roast it 30 to 35 minutes to the pound.

MINT APPLE DRESSING

2 cups croutons or all purpose stuffing
½ cup chopped apples
½ cup chopped mint
apple juice and lemon juice to moisten

Combine all ingredients and place in roasting pan as above.

BROCCOLI WITH CREAM CHEESE SAUCE

3 pounds broccoli

Wash, cook in boiling salted water just until tender. Serve with the following sauce.

CREAM CHEESE SAUCE

1 egg, beaten
3 ounces cream cheese
2 tablespoons lemon juice
paprika

Combine egg, cheese and lemon juice. Cook, stirring, over low heat in small saucepan until blended. If mixture becomes too thick, add extra lemon juice and garnish with paprika. Serve hot.

GREEN AND WHITE PARFAIT

½ -1 pint vanilla ice cream
½ -1 pint pistachio ice cream
crème de menthe

Into six parfait glasses place alternate layers of vanilla and pistachio ice cream. Place in freezer. Thirty minutes before serving, remove from freezer and pour 1 teaspoon crème de menthe over each parfait.

The parfaits may be assembled hours ahead. They will be ready to eat ½ hour after removing from freezer. They may also be garnished with whipped cream and green cherries.

Mrs Charles H.V. Talbot

Middle East Fare
(Serves 8)

Iranian Aubergines*
Cloved Rice*
Minted Peas*
Sour Cream Cucumbers*
Apricot Almond Soufflé*
Demi-tasse

IRANIAN AUBERGINES

4 small eggplants
6 - 8 tablespoons olive oil
½ cup onion, chopped
2 teaspoons salt
¼ teaspoon pepper
1 clove garlic, minced
2 cups ground beef or *lamb*
2 cups grapenut cereal
1 ½ cups tinned tomatoes, drained
2 eggs, slightly beaten

Cut eggplants in half lengthwise, scoop out centre leaving ½ inch thickness on skin. Parboil shells 5 minutes in salted water. Drain. Chop removed centres. Pour oil in large frying pan, heat and add chopped eggplant, onion, salt, pepper and garlic, and sauté. Add meat, 1 ½ cups grapenuts, tomatoes and eggs. Mix thoroughly. Fill shells. Sprinkle remaining grapenuts on top and bake at 400° F for 35 minutes.

CLOVED RICE

Cook 2 cups rice according to directions on package. But, before adding rice to water, add about a teaspoon of saffron and 10 or 12 whole cloves to water and salt. Unusual flavour and good accompaniment with above recipe. Peas may be added or served separately.

MINTED PEAS

2 packages frozen peas

Cook in very little salted water with a few grains of sugar, 1 tablespoon butter and several leaves of fresh mint, if desired.

SOUR CREAM CUCUMBERS

1 ½ teaspoons salt
1 ½ teaspoons sugar (scant)
3 tablespoons cider vinegar
1 ½ cups sour cream
2 tablespoons fresh dill
3 tablespoons chives, snipped
or grated onion
1 teaspoon celery seed
3 cucumbers, unpeeled

Dissolve salt and sugar in vinegar. Add sour cream. Stir until smooth. Add herbs and cucumbers, sliced thinly. Chill.

This could be served instead of the minted peas if plain peas were added to the cloved rice.

APRICOT ALMOND SOUFFLE

1 ½ cups dried apricot halves
¾ cup sugar (slightly less)
¾ cup boiling water
3 ounce package peach Jello
4 egg whites (at room temperature)
⅛ teaspoon cream of tartar
1 cup heavy cream
¾ teaspoon almond extract
3 tablespoons chopped toasted almonds

Put apricots in saucepan with 2 cups cold water and bring to boil. Simmer covered, until tender, about 25 minutes. Add sugar and cook additional 5 minutes. Cool. Sieve or blend apricots and liquid. Measure purée and if necessary add water to make 3 cups. Dissolve gelatin in boiling water. Mix thoroughly with purée. Cool about two hours, stirring occasionally. Mixture should be consistency of unbeaten egg white. Tie a collar of wax paper (buttered on inside) to form a rim 2 inches high around a quart and a half baking dish. Beat egg whites with cream of tartar until peaks form. Fold into mixture. Add almond extract to cream and fold gently into mixture. Pour into dish and refrigerate for at least 8 hours. Remove paper collar before serving. Press almonds evenly around raised sides of soufflé.

Mrs Phyllis West Harron

Dinner Party Fare
for Six

Onion Soup*
Beef Stroganoff*
Parsleyed Rice
Buttered Peas
Heart of Palm and Avocado Salad
Crème Brulée*

ONION SOUP

1 ½ cups onion, thinly sliced
3 tablespoons butter
6 cups beef (or chicken) broth
¼ teaspoon freshly ground pepper
6 slices French bread, toasted
1 cup Parmesan cheese, grated

Sauté onions in butter. Add broth and pepper. Cover and cook over low heat or in a 275° F oven for 30 minutes.

Now put in a casserole, cover with toast. Sprinkle cheese over the toast and heat for ten minutes. Add dash of Cognac or dry sherry, if desired.

BEEF STROGANOFF

3 pounds beef tenderloin cut into ¼-inch strips
2 jars mushrooms
3 to 4 onions
1 clove garlic
3 tablespoons butter and flour
1 cup beef broth
1 tablespoon tomato paste
8 ounces sour cream
½ cup sherry

Sauté mushrooms and onions. Remove. In same pan brown beef. Set aside.

Sauté garlic separately. Add butter and flour, then beef broth and tomato paste. Stir to make smooth sauce. Set aside.

Just before serving:
Add meat, mushrooms and onions to garlic mixture. Heat through and then add sour cream and sherry.

CREME BRULEE

2 cups heavy cream
4 eggs, beaten
2 tablespoons sugar
½ cup light brown sugar, approximately

Heat cream in double boiler until hot. Pour slowly over eggs. Return to double boiler and stir in sugar. Heat until custard coats spoon heavily. Pour into serving dish and chill well. Just before serving cover the custard with ¼ to ⅓ inch layer of light brown sugar. Heat in a 250° F oven until the sugar has caramelized. Chill.

Crème Brulée is best served as a topping for fresh fruit. I arrange the fruit in a dish and serve the custard in the centre.

Pat Thomson
Mrs Alan Thomson

Fisherman's Catch

Hashed Shark*
Mussel Pie*
Cherry Tomatoes
Garden Lettuce
Lemon Sherbet

HASHED SHARK
An old Bermudian favourite.

1 small cleaned shark
3 bunches finely chopped parsley
¼ cup finely chopped hot bird peppers

Wash shark and liver. Remove small green gall from liver as this is bitter. Fry liver over very low heat to extract oil.

Remove head and fins. Cut shark into steaks. Bring to boil in large pot- boil for approximately 20 minutes. Let cool.

When shark is cool remove skin and cartilage, squeeze out water with hands or cloth.

Cook parsley in liver oil approximately 10 minutes, add peppers and shark, continue to cook over low heat approximately 1 hour.

Helpful Hints:
You may choose to vary the amount of oil used according to personal preference and liver quality.

Allow 3-4 hours to prepare shark.

As the liver has an unpleasant smell it is a good idea if you have an electric fryer and extension cord to place the liver and fryer outside, cover and leave to cook.

Shark freezes very well.

Serving Suggestions:
Add a touch of mayonnaise for spreading on crackers - great with cocktails, on toast or out of a small bowl.

MUSSEL PIE

1 quart mussels (steamed and shelled)
2-3 potatoes (diced)
2 medium onions
Thyme to taste
¼ pound bacon
1 teaspoon vinegar
1 teaspoon soda
1 teaspoon curry

Cut up mussels, add one cup water and cook in pressure cooker for 5-8 minutes or simmer for 45 minutes to tenderize.

Chop onions and bacon, fry until brown and add to mussels with potatoes. Add thyme and stew until potatoes are almost tender. Add vinegar, soda and curry, complete cooking.

Place in deep casserole, cover with pastry and bake at 375° F until pastry is brown.

You may prefer to line your pan with pastry as well, as most mussel pie fans favour more pastry.

Can be prepared and frozen - cook when ready to serve. (Serves 4 to 5).

Carol M. West

Mrs Christopher West

❉ ❉ ❉ ❉ ❉ ❉ ❉ ❉ ❉

For dandruff, rub the scalp with lemon juice.

❉ ❉ ❉ ❉ ❉ ❉ ❉ ❉ ❉

Springtime Dinner
for Eight

Jellied Gazpacho Soup*
Chicken à la Greenway*
Rice and Roasted Almonds*
Carrot Mold with Green String Beans*
Dinner Rolls with Orange Butter*
Chilled Grapefruit Wedges*
Brownies*

JELLIED GAZPACHO SOUP

½ green pepper, cut into ½ inch pieces
1 large white onion, quartered
½ large unpared cucumber, cut into ½ inch pieces
1 large stalk celery, cut into ½ inch pieces
2 (13 ounces) tins madrilène consommé, well chilled
2 8-ounce containers plain yogurt
8 parsley sprigs for garnish
(8 wine or parfait stemmed glasses)

Combine pepper, onion, cucumber and celery in blender. Add enough water to cover. Blend at medium speed until just coarsely chopped. Pour into strainer and drain well. Combine chopped vegetables and madrilène in a bowl. Put layer of same into each wine glass. Put 2 tablespoons yogurt. Repeat layers, ending with topping of yogurt and a sprig of parsley. Serve very cold. Accompany with hot herb butter on water biscuits. (HOT HERB BUTTER: mix butter or margarine with oregano and chili powder to taste).

The Herb butter can be made the day before, as can the Gazpacho and the dessert!

CHICKEN A LA GREENWAY

2 fresh broilers, quartered
1 large lemon
8 tablespoons butter
8 tablespoons flour
1½ to 2 cups milk
2 1-pint boxes fresh mushrooms
1 small bunch white grapes
4 tablespoons cooking sherry
salt and ground white pepper

114

Rub the chicken parts with cut lemon, using all the juice. Put chicken in large pot. Add salt and partly cover chicken with cold water. Bring to a boil. Cover, turn down heat and cook until tender. Do not over cook. Put stock from chicken in bowl in refrigerator to set fat. (Dish can be prepared to this point day before).

Make a roux with butter or margarine and flour. Blend well in large double boiler. Slowly add milk. When cooked this makes a very thick cream sauce. Add enough stock (after removing fat) to make right consistancy for pouring. Cover.

Wash mushrooms thoroughly. Remove stems. Halve or quarter caps according to size. Drain on paper towelling. Wash grapes. Cut in half and remove seeds.

Skin and bone chicken in as large pieces as possible. Sauté mushrooms in 2 tablespoons butter and add to cream sauce. Add the sherry and season to taste. Fold in chicken pieces. Cover. Add white grapes just before serving.

RICE AND ROASTED ALMONDS

Boil Uncle Ben's rice following instructions on box. Add ½ cup chopped roasted almonds at last minute.

The rice may be serve separately or in cup-molds around large platter of the chicken. Garnish with finely chopped parsley and/or paprika.

CARROT MOLD WITH GREEN STRING BEANS

5 cups mashed cooked carrots
5 teaspoons minced onion
4 tablespoons melted margarine
4 eggs, well beaten
2 tablespoons flour
2 cups light cream or top milk
Salt, pepper and paprika to taste
1 ½ pounds young green beans

Fold all ingredients except beans together and pack into buttered 2-quart ring mold with open centre. Set in a shallow pan of hot water. Bake at 350° F until firm (50 to 70 minutes).

Cut washed young, green string beans into pea-sized pieces which should take not longer than 10 - 15 minutes to cook uncovered in salted boiling water. They should be slightly crisp and green. After turning out carrot mold on heated platter, drain beans and pour into centre of mold. Garnish carrot mold with plenty of paprika.

[Pumpkin may be substituted for carrots].

Serve with soft dinner rolls filled with orange butter. (ORANGE BUTTER:

mix ¾ stick butter or margarine with a little orange juice and finely grated orange peel). Serve very hot, but not dry.

CHILLED GRAPEFRUIT WEDGES

6 (preferably pink) seedless grapefruit

Use very sharp knife to remove skin and outside pulp. Cut out wedges from inside pulp sections. Place in shallow dish and macerate in either white wine, kirsch or Grand Marnier. Sprinkle with brown sugar, cover and refrigerate.

Serve in chilled glass fruit bowl and garnish with either maraschino cherries or freshly ground coconut.

BROWNIES (from old Bermudian receipt)

2 squares unsweetened chocolate
¼ cup butter
melt together in double boiler, remove from heat and add in following order, mixing after each addition:
1 cup white sugar
1 egg (unbeaten)
¾ teaspoon vanilla
½ cup white flour (scant)
½ cup chopped walnuts

Bake 20 minutes *only* in 375° F oven.

This receipt may be doubled for thicker, larger brownies. Cut into squares while still hot.

Janette R. Zuill

Mrs Vail Zuill

❀❀❀❀❀❀❀❀❀

To prevent falling hair, rub the head with salt and vinegar and the following day rub it with rum and sweet oil.

❀❀❀❀❀❀❀❀❀

Fisherman's Dinner

(Serves 8)

Baked Fish with Lemon-Rice Stuffing*
Onion, Tomato and Cucumber Salad with Dill Dressing*
Rum Cream Pie Williamsburg*
Demi-Tasse

BAKED FISH WITH LEMON-RICE STUFFING

5 - 6 pound fish for baking

Melt in a large frying pan:
⅓ cup butter or margarine

Add and cook until tender:
1 cup finely diced celery
½ cup chopped onions

Toss lightly with:
3-4 cups cooked rice
1 tablespoon grated lemon rind
½ teaspoon salt
¼ teaspoon fresh thyme or ground
¼ cup lemon juice

Sprinkle inside of washed fish lightly with salt. Stuff fish loosely, skewer and lace with coarse thread. Place on foil in baking pan, add melted butter or margarine. Wrap extra stuffing in foil and bake in pan. Bake for about 45 minutes to one hour, depending on thickness of fish. Serve fish with sliced ripe bananas sprinkled with lime juice and lemon quarters dipped in chopped parsley. This is an impressive dish particularly for visitors. Any vegetable may be served, especially pumpkin.

ONION, TOMATO AND CUCUMBER SALAD

Slice 2 white onions very thinly, slice tomatoes and cucumber. Add oil and vinegar dressing, sprinkle with chopped parsley and dill, capers or chives. Dressing should be tart.

RUM CREAM PIE WILLIAMSBURG (makes 2 8-inch pies)

2 graham cracker crusts
6 egg yolks
1 cup sugar
1 envelope gelatin
½ cup water

2 cups heavy cream, whipped
½ cup rum
bittersweet chocolate (or bitter)

Beat egg yolks and sugar together until light and fluffy. Soften gelatin in water until dissolved. Pour into egg mixture, beating briskly. Fold whipped cream into egg mixture, then add rum, carefully. Pour into graham cracker crusts and allow to set until firm in refrigerator. Before serving, grate chocolate on long blade to obtain swirls over top of pies.

Mrs Phyllis West Harron

❧

Chilean Dinner for Four

Avocado Stuffed with Shrimps
Dry White Wine
Chilean Meat Pie*
Claret
Fresh Fruit

CHILEAN MEAT PIE

1 medium onion, minced
2 cups leftover beef pot roast or lamb, cut up
10 pitted olives
2 hard-cooked eggs, chopped
1 teaspoon oregano
salt
⅛ teaspoon cayenne pepper
¼ cup canned condensed bouillon or consommé undiluted
1 can (20 ounces) cream style corn
2 eggs, well beaten
⅛ teaspoon pepper

Combine meat, onion, olives, oregano, salt, cayenne and bouillon. To corn add eggs, salt, pepper and mix well. Grease a 9-inch pie plate and put the meat mixture in, top with the corn mixture. Bake at 370° F for 45 minutes, then increase oven to 400° F and bake 15 minutes more. Remove from oven and cool for 10 minutes before serving.

Mrs Michael Marsh

Dinner At "Edey's Hill"

(Serves 8 to 10)

Chilled Tomato Consommé
Poularde Basquaise*
Brown or Wild Rice
Romaine and Avocado Salad
Alsatian Wine, chilled
Raspberry Snowball*

My favourite menu for either a dinner party or buffet supper. So much of this can be done ahead of time and for a maidless house it is one of the best!

POULARDE BASQUAISE

3 frying chickens
butter
bacon fat
¾ pound mushrooms, quartered
1 small eggplant, peeled and sliced in fingers
4 or 5 tomatoes, peeled and quartered
2 green peppers, sliced
2 cloves garlic, chopped and mashed
8 or 10 small white onions, cooked in butter for about 20 minutes
1 teaspoon basil
½ teaspoon dried thyme
2 bay leaves
1 or 2 truffles (optional)
salt and pepper
¾ cup white wine

Cut the chickens into quarters (*I sometimes use cut up chicken*). Brown pieces on all sides in half butter and half bacon fat. Add salt and pepper. Place the pieces of chicken in a casserole. In the fat in which the chickens were cooked, stir together the mushrooms, eggplant, tomatoes, green peppers, onion, garlic, thyme, bay leaves, basil and one or two truffles sliced. (They are expensive and not necessary). Add salt and pepper and place mixture around chicken in casserole. Pour ¾ cup of white wine into the first pan, stir and scrape to incorporate the brown bits and pour over chicken. Cover the casserole and cook in moderate oven (350° F) for 45 minutes.

RASPBERRY SNOWBALL

This can be made several days ahead!

¾ cup cold water
¾ cup granulated sugar
1 envelope unflavoured gelatin
¼ cup cold water
6 egg yolks
¼ cup light rum
2 cups heavy cream
3 pints raspberry sherbet
2 cups heavy cream

First make a rum mousse:
Into ¾ cup cold water, in saucepan, stir in the sugar until dissolved. Boil rapidly for 5 minutes - then cool this syrup without stirring. In measuring cup sprinkle the gelatin into ¼ cup cold water to soften; then set cup in simmering water and stir till gelatin is dissolved. In 1½ pint double boiler top with mixer at medium speed, beat the egg yolks till light; then beat in cooled syrup to blend. Cook and stir egg yolk mixture over simmering water until thickened, about 20 minutes. Remove from heat, stir in gelatin mixture then rum. Set the mixture in a bowl of ice cubes and stir constantly until cool, then gently fold it into the heavy cream, whipped. Place in refrigerator until just set.

In meantime, place a 2½ quart mixing bowl in freezer until well chilled. Using 3 pints of slightly softened sherbet, line the chilled bowl with ¾ inch of sherbet. Freeze it in the bowl till firm. Then fill it with the Rum Mousse, cover with foil, freeze.

Early on serving day unmold snowball by dipping mixing bowl in and out of very hot water, dry bowl, invert on serving plate. Again place in freezer. Whip 2 cups heavy cream very stiff. Ice the entire snowball with cream and again place in freezer until serving time.

If raspberry sherbet is unavailable I use orange sherbet and instead of rum in mousse I substitute Curaçao.

Clara Dill

Lady Dill

Patio Dinner
for Eight

Chicken Madrilène with Sour Cream and Red Caviar
Escalopes de veau à la crème flambées*
Tiny peas à l'oignon
Herbed Rice
Escarole Salad
Moselle Wine
Ice Cream with Fruit

ESCALOPES DE VEAU A LA CREME FLAMBEES
[*This recipe feeds eight people - takes 10 minutes to prepare*]

4 pounds veal cutlets, cut very thinly and then pounded with a
  bottle on a cutting board
½ pound butter
½ cup heavy cream
½ cup VERY HOT water
½ cup good brandy
seasonings to taste, such as salt, pepper, dry mustard, rosemary, dill,
garlic salt

Quickly brown veal in butter. Season and add *hot* water (cold will toughen) cover and simmer for ½ an hour at least. (you can simmer much longer if you want, or keep on a hot-tray) When all food is ready, and guests are seated, bring it out for the finale! Over a spirit lamp, heat brandy and flame it over the meat. Then stir in your heavy cream, and cook in front of your guests over the spirit lamp 2 more minutes: a chafing dish is ideal. (P.S. You can put away your knives this evening!)

Serve the veal with rice seasoned with chopped parsley, chives, paprika, salt, pepper and butter.

Mrs Gifford Stanton

Duckling Dinner

(Serves 8)

Honey Duckling*
Grand Marnier Sauce*
Ala Pilaf
Chinese Peapods
Salad*
Lime Chiffon Pie

HONEY DUCKLING

(Serves 4 - double for 8)

4 - 5 pound Long Island Duckling
Celery leaves
Onion
1 ½ cups dry white wine (Chablis preferred)
Honey

Remove the neck and other parts stored inside the duckling, wash thoroughly inside and out and dry it carefully. Fold the wings underneath to permit the duck to sit upright in the roasting pan. Rub the cavity with a piece of lemon adding celery leaves and an onion into the cavity. Place the bird breast up on a rack in a roasting pan. Preheat oven to 375° F cook for 30 minutes, reduce heat to 325° F and remove all fat from the pan with a syringe, retaining any juices if possible. Add 1½ cups of dry white wine and baste every 20 minutes for 1½ hours with wine pan juices. After duckling has roasted 1 hour and 40 minutes brush outer skin with honey and do not baste again. Cook for 20 minutes more then remove onion and celery leaves from cavity and discard. Cut duck into serving pieces with poultry shears and arrange on platter. Pan juices may be used as gravy or saved to make the sauce.

GRAND MARNIER SAUCE

1 tablespoon wine vinegar
½ cup sugar
Juice of 2 oranges
½ cup Grand Marnier
Grated orange rind
¼ cup julienne orange strips
12 mandarin orange sections

Cook sugar and wine vinegar over medium flame until sugar begins to caramelize. Add orange juice, Grand Marnier and orange rind, cook for 5 minutes and stir in pan juices. Add julienne orange strips and mandarin orange sections. Correct seasoning and pour part of sauce over duckling on serving platter, arranging orange slices decoratively. Pass remaining sauce.

SALAD

Toss fresh greens, tomatoes, cucumbers, onions, bits of real bacon (that have been frozen in jar in freezer for make ahead convenience), croutons, garlic and Parmesan. Add oil and vinegar dressing just before serving.

Jane Odenweller

Mrs Robert Odenweller

Spring Dinner for Eight

Roast Leg of Lamb basted with Honey
Broccoli Casserole*
Potato Boats
Mile High Ice Cream Pie*
Coffee or Tea

BROCCOLI CASSEROLE

1 stick (¼ pound) butter or margarine
1 roll garlic cheese or
  1 pound Cheddar cheese and garlic clove, minced
1 can (10 ¾ ounces) cream of mushroom soup
½ cup onions, chopped
1 small can mushrooms
2 packages frozen broccoli, cooked, drained, chopped
1 cup bread crumbs

Melt butter and add soup and cheese. Stir until melted. Add onions and mushrooms and broccoli. Stir in ½ cup of the bread crumbs. Place in a greased casserole. Top with remaining bread crumbs and dot with butter. Bake in 350° F oven until slightly browned. This will serve at least 8 and can be stretched further by adding another package of frozen broccoli. (Can be made ahead and frozen until needed. Thaw and heat through before serving).

MILE HIGH ICE CREAM PIE

1 baked 9-inch pie shell
2 pints ice cream (strawberry, chocolate, vanilla)

Meringue:
3 egg whites
6 tablespoons sugar
¼ teaspoon cream of tartar
½ teaspoon vanilla

Fill cool pie shell with layers of ice cream. Press down gently so as not to break the crust. Make the meringue (beat egg whites until stiff, adding sugar gradually with cream of tartar and vanilla). Cover the ice cream with the meringue, being sure to seal to edges. Put into a preheated 450° F oven for 3-5 minutes or until lightly browned. *Watch carefully*. Freeze the pie. Serve with chocolate sauce or strawberries spooned over each slice as you cut it. It is easier to cut if taken from the freezer about 20 minutes before serving. Should be made the day before.

This is a very easy recipe and is always a success.

Mrs Richard Gibbons

Jordy's Garden Dinner

(Serves 6)

Avocado Soup
Pork Tenderloin with Orange Sauce*
Paw paw, Tomato and Cheese Bake
Steamed Zucchini
Citrus Alaska*

PORK TENDERLOIN WITH ORANGE SAUCE

Tie up tenderloin so that it doesn't come apart during cooking.
Put in baking dish and cover with orange juice. Bake at 300° F basting occasionally until done. Remove from baking dish and keep hot in oven while making sauce. In baking dish, make roux using butter and whole wheat flour. Add orange juice and drippings from the cooking. Add as much fresh orange juice as necessary, to make sauce desired consistency.
Serve sauce piping hot, in gravy boat.

CITRUS ALASKA

Halve 3 grapefruits and scoop out pulp. Peel grapefruits and oranges and cut out sections, removing all skin and white pulp. Partially fill grapefruit halves with citrus and some juice. Add some Grand Marnier. Make meringue and cover grapefruit halves with this, sealing edges.

Place under broiler for a few minutes. Serve immediately.

Mary Walker

Mrs B.W. Walker

Southampton Supper for Six
Bacon and Egg Pie*
Coleslaw
Stuart's Special Dessert*

BACON AND EGG PIE

An English dish served for tea.

Two crust pastry
¾ pound chopped bacon
4 eggs, beaten
1 tablespoon grated onion
1 tablespoon grated potato
salt and pepper to taste

Mix all ingredients together and pour into unbaked pie shell. Cover with pastry top and cut slits to allow steam to escape. Brush top with egg or milk. Bake at 425° F for 15 minutes, then reduce temperature to 350° F and bake for 30-35 minutes.

Delicious served hot or cold.

STUART'S SPECIAL DESSERT

Put a scoop of chocolate ice cream into six individual dessert dishes. Drizzle crème de menthe over top. Then top with chocolate sauce and whipped cream. Sprinkle liberally with chopped nuts.

Elizabeth Parker

Mrs Geoffrey Parker

Harvest Feast
(Serves 8 to 10)

Cream of Pumpkin Soup*
Pork Tenderloin "en croute"*
Broccoli with Lemon Butter
Garden Carrots
Vin Rosé
Strawberries n' Cream Special*

CREAM OF PUMPKIN SOUP

4 pounds pumpkin (peeled and cubed)
1 ½ pounds potatoes (peeled and cubed)
3 large tomatoes (quartered and seeded)
1 large onion (peeled and quartered)
1 Chourico hot sausage (cut in three)
3 ½ -4 cups water
Salt and pepper
2 tablespoons butter
½ cup light cream

Place the pumpkin, potatoes, tomatoes, onion, sausage and water into a saucepan and bring to the boil. Reduce the heat, add the seasonings and simmer until tender (about 25 minutes).

Remove from the heat and purée soup in a blender or pass through a sieve.

Return to a saucepan and heat gently until ready to serve, at which time add the cream and stir in the butter until melted. Serve with warm croutons.

This soup may be made ahead of time and frozen, omitting the butter and cream which can be added when ready to serve.

PORK TENDERLOIN "EN CROUTE"

3 large pork tenderloins (about 5-6 pounds in all)
1 pound puff pastry
Parsley (for garnish)

Filling:
2 medium-size onions (chopped)
2 ounces (¼ cup) butter
½ pound mushrooms (finely chopped)
1 apple (grated)
2 tablespoons chopped sage
3 tablespoons chopped parsley

6-8 ounces cooked ham (chopped)
1 ½ cups fresh breadcrumbs
Pork trimmings (finely chopped)
1 egg (beaten)

To prepare the tenderloins:-
Trim and discard any fat. Finely chop meat trimmings and reserve for filling.
Cut each tenderloin in half lengthwise and set aside (six pieces in all).

To prepare the filling:-
Slowly melt the butter in a pan, add the onions to soften, then add the mushrooms together with the herbs. Cover and cook for about 5 minutes.
Draw pan off the heat, add breadcrumbs, apple and chopped ham. Turn into a bowl to cool then stir in the meat trimmings and ½ beaten egg. Season to taste.
Using half the filling, layer three tenderloin pieces together. Repeat with the remaining filling and three tenderloin pieces. Tie each of the layered tenderloins neatly to hold their shape during cooking.
Bake in a hot oven at 425° F for 1 ¼ hours, basting frequently. Leave the meat to go quite cold, then remove the strings. Reserve the pan drippings for the sauce.
Roll out half the pastry into a large rectangle and set one of the prepared tenderloins on it. Dampen the outside edges and cover the meat with the pastry. Tuck in the ends and seal all edges firmly. Brush with beaten egg and decorate with fleurons. Roll out the remaining pastry and cover the second tenderloin similarly.
Set the two tenderloins on a dampened baking sheet and cook in oven at 425° F for about 30 minutes (until well browned).
Place on serving dish and garnish with parsley. Slice and serve with a brown sauce, made from the pan drippings.
This dish may be prepared ahead of time and refrigerated (for one day) or frozen after the tenderloins have been covered with pastry. When required, remove freezer wrapping, allow to thaw, then bake for 30 minutes as directed. It is preferable to brush the tenderloins with the beaten egg after they have been thawed and prior to baking.

STRAWBERRIES N' CREAM SPECIAL

1 6-ounce packet chocolate chips
¾ cup Cointreau
1 ½ quarts fresh strawberries (washed and hulled)
1 cup double cream (whipped and sweetened to taste)
1 pint (approximately) vanilla ice cream (beaten until soft)

Melt the chocolate chips slowly over hot water then spread evenly on waxed paper to make a large square. Leave to set. When set cut carefully into 10 squares and carefully peel off the paper. Cut each square in half diagonally and set aside.

Crush ¼ of the strawberries in a bowl, sprinkle with sugar and stir in Cointreau. Cover and chill.

When ready to serve, mix whipped cream with beaten ice-cream and stir in chilled crushed strawberry mixture. Layer cream mixture with the remaining whole strawberries into individual parfait glasses, finishing with a layer of cream. Top each serving decoratively with two chocolate triangles and serve immediately.

Deanna M. Moss

Mrs Thomas Moss

"Brimstone Hill" Dinner
(Serves 6-8)

Cheese Treats*
Cream Cheese Soup
Pork Tenderloin à la Brimstone Hill*
Winlo's Pineapple Cream Surprise*

CHEESE TREATS

½ cup margarine (not butter)
½ pound grated cheese (sharp)
1 cup flour

Cream margarine and cheese....gradually add flour....form into a ball and put in refrigerator over night. Following day take out by teaspoonfuls and make into small balls. Cook 20 minutes (or golden brown) on ungreased cookie sheet at 350° F.
Yeild: approximately 40 cheesies

PORK TENDERLOIN A LA BRIMSTONE HILL

3 pork tenderloins (approximately 3 ½ -4 pounds)
2 eggs, beaten
bread crumbs
salt and pepper
butter for browning

Dip the tenderloins in the beaten eggs, roll in bread crumbs then brown in butter. Season with salt and pepper.

Sauce:
1 large can (14 ½ ounces) tomatoes
¼ cup vinegar
½ cup brown sugar
1 teaspoon allspice
1 teaspoon cloves

Combine all ingredients and boil for three minutes. Pour over the tenderloins and bake, covered, for three hours at 300° F.

WINLO'S PINEAPPLE CREAM SURPRISE

Pastry:
2 ¼ cups graham cracker crumbs
½ cup butter, melted
¼ cup brown sugar, optional

Mix ingredients until well combined and press into an 8-inch square baking dish or 9-inch pie plate. Bake at 300° F for 15 minutes. Cool.

Filling:
½ cup butter
2 cups icing sugar
2 eggs

Combine ingredients and beat until fluffy. Pour into cooled pie crust and chill until firm.

Topping:
1 cup cream, whipped
1 cup crushed pineapple, drained
¼ cup graham cracker crumbs

Fold pineapple into whipped cream. Spoon over chilled pie filling and sprinkle with crumbs. Chill until ready to serve. This is very rich....I often make a small crust and half the recipe.

Jaull Drew

Mrs Michael Drew

❋❋❋❋❋❋❋❋❋

Drink fried onion juice to help a cough.

❋❋❋❋❋❋❋❋❋

Mid-night Supper
at
"Highclere Cottage"

(Serves 12 or more)

Almond Cheese Roll*
Red Bean Soup*
Ham with Red Currant Glaze*

ALMOND-CHEESE ROLL

[*To serve with drinks*]

Sauté until golden brown, then chop finely:
1 cup blanched almonds in
3 tablespoons butter

Cream together:
3 ounces cream cheese
½ pound sharp Cheddar cheese, grated

Add almonds to cheese. Then add:
1 pimento, chopped
1 tablespoon lemon juice
1 ½ teaspoons salt
1 teaspoon Worcestershire sauce
2 teaspoons finely chopped onion
dash paprika

Mix well. Shape into two rolls. Roll in chopped toasted almonds.
  Wrap in foil. (Can be prepared two days in advance and refrigerated, or considerably in advance and frozen.) To serve, defrost and cut into thin slices and serve with crackers.

RED BEAN SOUP

Cover with water and boil for 1 hour:
1 box (1 pound) Red Kidney Beans

Add:
Ham bone
3 large potatoes, diced
2 Portuguese hot sausages, sliced

paprika
pepper and salt
1 tablespoon vinegar
thyme
2 large onions, diced
1 tin tomato soup (or 1 small tin tomato paste)

Add more water to cover and simmer for about 6 hours, or until reduced and thickening. Store in refrigerate or freezer.

RED-CURRANT GLAZE FOR HAM

Here's a glaze for ham a bit different, but very easy!

Heat and stir ½ cup currant jelly with 2 teaspoons sherry until jelly melts. Fifteen minutes before end of baking time, set oven to 350° F and spoon half glaze over ham, basting several times with remaining glaze.

FLUFFY MUSTARD

Beat with whisk;
2 egg yolks

Add:
1 tablespoon sugar
2 tablespoons prepared French mustard
1 tablespoon prepared hot mustard
2 tablespoons vinegar
1 tablespoon water
¾ teaspoon salt

Mix well. Cook over HOT, NOT BOILING water, stirring constantly until mixture thickens, about 5 to 7 minutes. Remove from heat; blend in:
1 tablespoon butter or margarine
1 tablespoon prepared horseradish

Refrigerate until thoroughly cool.

Fold in:
½ cup whipping cream, whipped.

Store in refrigerator. [*To serve with warm meat, remove from refrigerator 30 minutes ahead*]. Makes about 1 ⅓ cups.

Serving Suggestion: Buffet style
Self-service of soup from tureen. Arrange sliced ham on platter and serve sliced French loaf for sandwiches if desired. Fluffy mustard is good here

with a variety of pickles and your favourite condiments. A great snack for New Year's Eve after celebrations as everything can be prepared in advance!

Judi Davidson

Mrs Alan Davidson

Friday Night Dinner for Six

Watercress Soup*
Baked Hogfish*
Christophines in butter
Apricot Fool*

WATERCRESS SOUP

1 large bunch watercress
1 ounce (2 tablespoons) butter
1 ½ pints (3 cups) water
salt and pepper
1 egg yolk
¼ pint (½ cup) fresh cream

Wash watercress, chop finely, stew gently in melting butter for 3 minutes. Add water, simmer for 10 minutes. Season well. Remove from heat and add egg yolk beaten with cream and whisk well. Reheat gently for 3 minutes.

BAKED HOGFISH

4 pounds hogfish fillets
1 tablespoon olive oil
salt and pepper
lemon juice
½ pound sliced fresh mushrooms
4 medium onions
parsley
1 cup white wine
Fresh bread crumbs

Place fillets in buttered casserole, sprinkle with olive oil, season with salt and pepper and lemon juice, add mushrooms. Chop onions and parsley finely, add with wine to casserole. Cover with breadcrumbs and bake in a moderate oven (350° F) for 40-45 minutes.

APRICOT FOOL

½ pound dried apricots
2 tablespoon lemon juice
12 tablespoons water
4 ounces (½ cup) sugar
½ pint (1 cup) thick custard sweetened and cooled
½ pint (1 cup) cream

Simmer apricots with water, lemon juice and sugar until soft. Place in blender until smooth using more water if necessary. Add prepared custard and blend together. Whisk cream until thick, slowly add apricot mixture to cream. Pour into small glass dishes and chill. Serve with cream and almond flakes.

Margaret Parsons

Mrs John Parsons

"Below Deck" Dinner
(Serves 6)

Conch Fritters*
Bumble's Best Chicken Tarragon*
White Rice
Chicory and Tomato Salad
Pug's Coffee Soufflé*

CONCH FRITTERS

3 conchs
2 stalks celery
1 green pepper
2 small onions
1 egg, beaten
2 cups flour
1 teaspoon baking powder
salt, pepper and thyme

Grind conchs, celery, green pepper and onion in meat grinder; add egg, flour, baking powder, seasoning and water to make a drop batter. Drop teaspoonful at a time into hot deep fat. When browned, remove and drain on paper towel. Serve hot.

BUMBLE'S BEST CHICKEN TARRAGON

5 pounds chicken pieces
seasoning salt (I use Lawry's)
tarragon
chicken broth
sour cream, large carton

Place the chicken pieces in a baking dish, cover with chicken broth, season with the salt and tarragon. Bake in a 400° F oven for 1 hour, basting while cooking. Remove the chicken to a serving platter. Add the sour cream to the remaining broth, stirring to make a smooth sauce. Pour over the chicken pieces, and serve.

PUG'S COFFEE SOUFFLE

¾ cup boiling water
⅔ cup sugar
½ cup milk
¼ cup water with an envelope of unflavored gelatin
    dissolved in it
2 heaping teaspoons of instant coffee
3 eggs, separated

In the top of a double boiler, place the water, coffee, ⅓ cup of sugar, milk and the water with gelatin. Mix the other ⅓ cup of sugar with the egg yolks. Add this to the hot mixture.
  Cool to room temperature. Beat the egg whites till stiff and fold into the mixture. Pour into a soufflé dish and place in refrigerator till set, approximately 4 - 6 hours or over night.

Hope S. Berg

Mrs John Berg

Family Night Dinner

(Serves 6-8)

Pork and Sauerkraut Casserole*
Buttered New Potatoes
Mocha Mallow Mould*

PORK AND SAUERKRAUT CASSEROLE

2 pounds pork shoulder, cut in 1½-inch pieces
2 tablespoons salad oil

1 cup sliced carrots
1 large onion, chopped
1 tablespoon salt
1 bay leaf
¼ teaspoon pepper
4 cups sauerkraut, well drained (1 27-ounce can)
2 apples, cut in 1 ½ -inch pieces
½ cup apple juice
2 tablespoons chopped parsley
1 tabelspoon light brown sugar

About two hours before serving:
In Dutch oven over medium-high heat, in hot oil, brown pork well on all sides; add 1 cup water, carrots, onion, salt, bay leaf and pepper. Reduce heat to low; simmer, covered 1½ hours or until meat is fork-tender.

Add sauerkraut, apples, apple juice, chopped parsley and light brown sugar; cook, covered, 15 minutes more or until apples are tender and sauerkraut is heated through. Serve on large, warm platter.

MOCHA MALLOW MOULD

2 dessertspoonfuls gelatin
3 tablespoonsful liquid coffee
¼ pint (½ cup) hot water
4 ounces (20) marshmallows
4 ounces plain chocolate, coarsely chopped
½ pint (1 cup) evaporated milk
optional - 12 bourbon biscuits
¼ pint (½ cup) whipped cream

Soften gelatin in coffee and put into basin over pan of boiling water. Add hot water and the marshmallows and chocolate. Cook and stir frequently until marshmallows and chocolate have melted and mixture is smooth. Leave in cold place until just beginning to thicken. Whisk the evaporated milk until thickened and gradually add to the marshmallow mixture. (Add a little brandy if you like). Pour into an oiled cake tin and leave to set. Turn the mould out and press halved bourbon biscuits around the sides with a little whipped cream and decorate the top with cream.

Brenda Spearing

Mrs Alfred Spearing

Round the World Dinner

(Serves 8)

Quiche Lorraine
Veal Steak
German Fries*
Scalloped Lima Beans*
Texas Fruit Salad*

GERMAN FRIES

Use one large onion to each large potato. Cut onions and potatoes into thin slices. Put lots of bacon fat in fry pan. Layer the onions and potatoes in pan. Add salt and small amount of pepper to each layer. Fry slowly turning as they brown.

Also good cold with French dressing.

SCALLOPED LIMA BEANS

1 package frozen baby lima beans (cook as directed on package)
Sauté in 2 tablespoons butter:
1 small green pepper, chopped and 1 small onion, chopped.

Cream sauce:-
1 tablespoon butter
1 tablespoon flour
(blend over low heat)
add 1 cup milk and stir for 5 minutes.
add 1 cup grated cheese (Cheddar or Cracker Barrel)
Keep over heat only until cheese has melted.
Add lima beans, pepper and onions to cream sauce.
1 cup soft bread crumbs.

Put layer of crumbs in buttered casserole. Then layer of beans and then sauce mixture. Continue layers ending with sauce. Put remaining crumbs on top. Bake at 325° F for ½ hour.

TEXAS FRUIT SALAD

2 cans mandarin oranges
2 cups miniature marshmallows
2 bunches small green seedless grapes

Combine with heavy whipped cream (fresh dairy). 2 tablespoons sugar and 1 teaspoon vanilla per ¼ pint.

Mrs Bea White

My Favourite Dinner Menu

(for 6 to 8)

Consommé
Roast Pork with Sherry*
Baked Pumpkin
Oven-Browned Potatoes
Salad
Apple Muffins*
Ice Cream Pie with Fruit*
Coffee

ROAST PORK WITH SHERRY

5 to 6 pound boned and rolled pork roast
Sherry
Bottled sweet-and-sour sauce

If pork is frozen, defrost. Marinate in sherry for twelve hours. Put pork and marinade in roasting pan and bake at 350° F for 2½ hours. Baste roast with sweet and sour sauce and continue roasting for 30 minutes. Remove roast from pan and make gravy from drippings, adding bouillon or more sherry if needed.

APPLE MUFFINS (compliments of Mary Tucker)

¾ cup and 2 tablespoons milk
1 egg
⅓ cup liquid shortening
½ cup sugar
1 apple (cored, peeled and quartered)
2 cups flour
2 teaspoons baking powder
1¼ teaspoons baking soda
½ teaspoon salt

Mix first five ingredients in blender. Sift flour, baking powder, soda and salt together and add to liquid. Stir lightly. Put in greased muffin pan and bake at 400° F for 25 minutes
  Makes one dozen muffins.

ICE CREAM PIE WITH FRUIT

1 baked pie shell
1 large can peaches
1 3-ounce package orange Jello
1 pint vanilla ice cream
1 small can peach slices

Strain peaches from large can and reserve liquid to make one cup. Add water to liquid if necessary. Mash peaches and measure one cup. Heat peach juice to just under boiling. Add orange Jello and stir with wooden spoon until dissolved. Remove from heat (this is important) and add ice cream by the tablespoon to hot liquid quickly until ice cream is melted. Blend in peach pulp and mix well. Chill in saucepan until mixture is thickened a little but not completely set (about 25 minutes). Turn into baked pie shell, top with sliced peaches - one in the middle and one for every slice you will cut.

Any flavor Jello or fruit may be used in this recipe. Orange Jello is lovely with appricots, lemon Jello with strawberries.

Frances Clark

Mrs David E. Clark

⚜

Dinner at "Bayswater Cottage"

(Serves 6-8)

Split Pea Soup with Croutons
Stuffed Leg of Veal
Parsleyed New Potatoes
Spinach Casserole*
Garden Carrots
Rolls
English Trifle*

SPINACH CASSEROLE

2 packages frozen chopped spinach
8 ounces cream cheese
8 tablespoons butter
Salt and pepper
¾ cup Pepperidge Farm stuffing
(or breadcrumbs and sage)

Cook and drain spinach and put in buttered casserole. Stir in 4 tablespoons of butter and the cream cheese. Melt other 4 tablespoons butter in saucepan and toss with stuffing. Sprinkle over spinach. Bake in 350° F oven for 30 minutes. Can be prepared ahead of time and heated.

ENGLISH TRIFLE

Birds' Custard
(Make with 1 pint milk according to instructions on tin.)
1 package lady fingers (or sponge cake)
1 medium can of sliced peaches
strawberry jam
Chopped walnuts
Sherry

Crumble (coarsely) 2-3 lady fingers in bottom of dessert dish. Arrange peach slices over this and add a little of the juice. Put dabs of strawberry jam on top, sprinkle lightly with nuts. Sprinkle sherry over all - liberally! Pour custard to cover completely. Repeat above 2-3 times more making sure last layer of custard covers all ingredients. Most successful when made the day before and chilled.

Before serving cover with whipped cream and decorate with nuts and cherries.

Jean M. Cooper

Mrs Forster Cooper

St. Nicholas's Day Dinner for Six
(6 December)

*Kir**
Palourdes Farcies*
(stuffed clams)
Navarin aux pommes*
(lamb stew with potatoes)
Châteauneuf-du-pape
Tarte à l'orange*
(fresh orange pie)

KIR

Pour one tablespoon of "crème de cassis" into a chilled wine glass and fill the glass with a chilled white Burgundy wine.

PALOURDES FARCIES

24 clams (checkerboard or others)
salt, pepper
5 tablespoons butter
½ cup parsley, chopped
3 cloves garlic, minced
2 shallots, finely chopped

Open the clams, rinse under running water to remove sand and discard one shell from each. Loosen the meat from the remaining shell but leave in shell. Put the clams on a baking sheet. Salt and pepper lightly. Combine the remaining ingredients (the quantities may be varied to taste). Place a generous amount of this mixture on top of each clam. Just before serving run under a heated broiler for 3 or 4 minutes (until bubbling). May be prepared and kept (covered) an hour or so before broiling.

NAVARIN AUX POMMES

3.½ pounds lamb shoulder
1 large onion, chopped
3 cloves garlic, crushed
3 tablespoons flour
4 tomatoes, peeled and seeded
salt and pepper
"bouquet garni"
2 cups dry white wine
Stock
12 potatoes, peeled

Cut meat into serving pieces and brown a few at a time in oil in a skillet. Remove to a heat-proof casserole. Brown the onion and add to the meat. Also add the garlic, flour and tomatoes. Season and add the "bouquet garni" (parsley sprigs, thyme, bay leaf and cloves tied together). Mix well and add the wine and enough stock to cover meat. Bring to a boil and cook covered about 1½ hours (until meat is tender).

Place the potatoes in another oven-proof casserole with 2 tablespoons butter (or 1 tablespoon butter and 1 tablespoon chicken fat). Add stock to cover. Season. Bake in oven (350° F) covered about 45 minutes (until potatoes are done and the liquid is absorbed).

Remove the meat when done and keep warm. Pour off excess fat from the sauce and remove the "bouquet garni". If the sauce is too liquid, reduce it by boiling and stirring a few minutes.

To serve the "navarin", arrange the potatoes on a platter. Cover with the meat and pour the sauce over all. Sprinkle with chopped parsley.

TARTE A L'ORANGE

Baked 9-inch pie crust
1 cup orange marmalade
3 or 4 fresh navel oranges
2 tablespoons orange liqueur (optional)

Melt orange marmalade over low heat. Paint inside of pie crust with melted marmalade. Arrange orange sections decoratively in crust. Pour orange marmalade over all. Just before serving, sprinkle with sugar and run under a broiler to caramelize. Pour warmed orange liqueur on top and bring to the table flaming. This is a very refreshing and light dessert but to be successful the oranges must be excellent - tree-ripened, if possible.

Margaret de Marcy

Mrs Hubert de Marcy

Intimate Dinner Party For 4

Avocado Soup*
Veal with Fines Herbes*
Green Beans
Noodles with Garlic
Walnuts and Endive Salad*
Lemon Dainty

AVOCADO SOUP

2 ripe avocado pears
1 teaspoon curry powder
Salt
Freshly ground pepper
¼ pint (½ cup) double cream
1 pint (2 cups) stock
2 teaspoons lemon juice
Cayenne pepper
Finely chopped parsley

Peel avocados thinly and halve lengthwise; remove stones and dice flesh, retaining a little of the darker green flesh for garnish. Blend diced avocado in an electric blender with the curry powder, salt and freshly ground black pepper, and double cream. Combine stock and lemon juice. Bring gently to a boil; add a little to the avocado and cream mixture, and then blend all together with the remaining stock and reheat gently. Correct seasoning, adding a little cayenne pepper, and more lemon juice if desired. Serve in individual dishes, garnished with chunks of dark green avocado and a little finely chopped parsley.

VEAL WITH FINES HERBES

2 pounds veal scallops
Butter for cooking
1 cup white wine
Chives, tarragon, chervil, parsley

Sauté about two pounds veal scallops in butter and arrange on heatproof dish. To remaining pan juices add wine. Cook over high heat till wine is reduced by half.

Add chives, tarragon, chervil and parsley. Swirl in 2 good tablespoons butter and pour the sauce over the meat.

WALNUTS AND ENDIVE SALAD

Wash endives thoroughly and cut up into bite size pieces. Add walnuts and dressing.

Gill's Dressing
1 cup Italian olive oil
½ cup tarragon vinegar
juice of 1 lemon
1 tablespoon Dijon mustard
Salt
Pepper
Parsley
Fines Herbes
A little watercress, if available
Mix all ingredients in blender.

Gill Reiss

Mrs. Fred Reiss

Sunday Supper
"en famille"
(Serves 6)

Chicken Casserole*
Fire & Ice Tomatoes*
Southern Corn Pone*
Lime-Mint Sherbet*
Meringue Kisses*

CHICKEN CASSEROLE

4 chicken breasts
1 cup mushrooms, sliced
4 tablespoons butter
4 tablespoons flour
1 can cream of chicken soup
1 cup milk
1 cup chicken broth (from stewing the chicken)
½ package Pepperidge Farm herbed stuffing

Stew the chicken breasts. Cool in their broth. Remove skin and bones and cut the meat in large cubes. Sauté mushrooms in butter. Add flour and blend well. Add soup, milk and broth. Cook until thick. Arrange in greased casserole in three layers: 1st chicken, 2nd sauce, 3rd stuffing; Bake 350° F for 30 minutes.

FIRE & ICE TOMATOES

6 firm ripe tomatoes, skinned, sliced or quartered
1 green pepper, sliced
1 onion in rings

Place in a bowl.
Sauce:
¾ cup vinegar
¼ cup water
1 ½ teaspoons celery salt
1 ½ teaspoons mustard seed
½ teaspoon salt
4 ½ teaspoons sugar
⅛ teaspoon red pepper
⅛ teaspoon black pepper

Boil for 1 minute and while still hot pour over tomatoes, pepper and onion. Cool. Just before serving add 1 peeled and sliced cucumber. Serve as relish or side dish.

SOUTHERN CORN PONE (Modern adaptation)

2 cups corn meal
½ cup sugar
¼ cup butter
3 cups boiling water
3 eggs, beaten
1½ cups milk
1 tablespoon salt, scant

Pour boiling water over dry ingredients. Add milk, butter and mix well until smooth. Add eggs. Pour mixture in well greased 8 inch square pan 2 inches deep. Bake at 350° F for one hour.

This is not the usual dry, crumbly corn bread. Tis moist and fine grained, like the old mammies used to make in the Deep South, baking it a longer time in slow oven of wood-burning range. Excellent made with the fine yellow West Indian corn meal available in Bermuda.

LIME-MINT SHERBET

10 sprigs fresh mint
2 cups water
¾ cup sugar
½ cup white corn syrup
2 teaspoons grated lime rind
½ cup lime juice

2 drops green food colouring
2 egg whites, stiffly beaten

Wash, dry and chop mint leaves picked from the stems. Add water and sugar. Bring to a boil. Stir until sugar dissolves. Cool and strain. Add corn syrup, lime rind and juice. Add colouring. Freeze in refrigerator tray until firm. Remove to mixing bowl, break up mixture and beat with electric beater until mushy and smooth. Fold in the egg whites and freeze until firm.

MERINGUE KISSES

2 egg whites
1 cup sugar
⅛ teaspoon salt
½ teaspoon almond or vanilla extract
1 teaspoon grated lemon or lime rind

Beat egg whites until stiff. Add sugar and salt slowly, beating constantly. Gently fold in flavouring and grated rind. Drop from a spoon onto lightly greased cookie sheet. Bake 25 to 30 minutes at 275° F.

Frances R. Burton

Frances R. Burton for Mrs Warren Brown

Elegant Dinner For Six

Scallops au gratin*
dry white wine
Else's Filet Mignon Parmesan*
French Fried Potatoes
Asparagus & Hollandaise Sauce*
Red Burgundy or Bordeaux
Hot Rolls & Butter
Chocolate Bavarian Cream*

SCALLOPS AU GRATIN

This recipe may be made in advance and browned just before serving.

1 medium onion, chopped
1 ounce (2 tablespoons) butter
1 garlic clove, chopped

Cook the onions slowly in butter in small saucepan for 5 minutes until tender but not browned. Stir in garlic and cook slowly for 1 minute more. Set aside.

30 medium-sized scallops, washed
Salt and pepper
4 ounces (1 cup) flour
2 tablespoons butter
1 tablespoon olive oil
¼ cup dry white vermouth
½ bay leaf
⅛ teaspoon thyme
½ cup Swiss cheese, grated

Dry the scallops and cut into ¼ inch thick slices. Just before cooking, sprinkle with salt and pepper, roll in flour, and shake off excess. Then sauté the scallops quickly in 2 tablespoons butter and 1 tablespoon olive oil to brown them lightly.

Pour ¼ cup dry white vermouth and 4 tablespoons water into the pan with the scallops. Add ½ bay leaf and ⅛ teaspoon thyme, and the cooked onion mixture. Cover pan and simmer for 5 minutes. Then uncover, and if necessary boil down the sauce rapidly for a minute until it is lightly thickened. Correct seasoning and discard bay leaf.

Spoon scallops and sauce into scallop shells. Sprinkle with grated Swiss cheese and dot with butter.

Just before serving, place under hot grill for 3 to 4 minutes to heat through and brown cheese lightly.

ELSE'S FILET MIGNON PARMESAN

6 beef fillets about 2-inches thick
Garlic
Salt and pepper
6 tablespoons grated Parmesan cheese
3 eggs
6 tablespoons milk
3 tablespoons red wine
bread crumbs

Pound fillets until they are about 1-inch thick. Rub with garlic, salt and pepper, and pat in Parmesan cheese. (May be prepared ahead of time to this point). Beat eggs and milk, and add wine. Dip steaks into this liquid, then roll in bread crumbs and sauté in heavy frying pan in equal parts of oil and butter 3 - 4 minutes each side for rare. Do not pierce fillets in turning, as the cheese holds the juices.

Sauce:
Sauté equal parts of chopped onions and mushrooms in oil and butter

and a little parsley. When soft, add enough heavy cream just to bind together. Serve on top of steaks.

ASPARAGUS WITH HOLLANDAISE SAUCE

Cook two packages of frozen asparagus spears as directed on package and serve with Hollandaise Sauce.

Hollandaise Sauce:
This can be made ahead of time and kept warm by setting container in a saucepan containing 2-inches of hot water.

Melt ½ pound (1 cup) butter

Into blender container put:
4 eggs yolks
2 tablespoons lemon juice
1 teaspoon salt
Pinch cayenne

Cover container and turn motor on low speed. *Immediately* remove cover and pour in the hot butter in a steady stream. When all butter is added, turn off motor.

CHOCOLATE BAVARIAN CREAM

Into blender container put:
2 envelopes plain gelatin
¼ cup cold water
½ cup hot milk or strong coffee

Cover and blend on high speed for 40 seconds. Then add:
1 package (6 ounces) semisweet chocolate chips
¼ cup sugar

Cover and blend on high speed for 10 seconds. Remove cover and, with motor on, add:
2 egg yolks
1 cup heavy cream
1 heaping cup crushed ice

Continue to blend for 20 seconds longer, than pour into 1 large 4-cup mold or into individual molds.
Serve with whipped cream.

Trudy Pool

Mrs Clive Pool

A Hearty Man's Dinner
(Serves Six to Eight)

Borscht*
Steak & Kidney Pie*
Fleurie
PawPaw au gratin*
Green Salad Vinaigrette
Chocolate/Orange Mousse *
Sauternes

Everything but salad can be made day before.

BORSCHT

1 quart beef broth or canned consommé
2 cups raw beets, peeled and chopped
  (or shredded)
1 onion, chopped
1-2 cups shredded cabbage
1 tablespoon vinegar or lemon juice
½ cup sour cream

Put beef broth, beets, onion and cabbage in a pan and simmer, covered, until vegetables are tender. Put in blender until smooth. Add vinegar or lemon juice and water to make 1½ quarts. Taste and season further if necessary. Serve hot or chilled with spoonful sour cream in centre of each bowlful.

STEAK AND KIDNEY PIE

2 ½-3 pounds pie beef
½ pound lamb kidneys
4 tablespoons flour
½ cup butter or margarine
2 onions
2 cups water or beef broth

Trim beef and cut into small pieces. Cut core from kidneys and chop very small. Put all meat in bag with flour and seasoning and shake to coat. Melt fat in large skillet and add meat, turning frequently until brown on all sides. Slice onions and add, pour on 2 cups water or beef broth. C   and simmer gently for 2 - 3 hours taking care not to let meat bottom of pan. Add more liquid if necessary. When tender re
inch pie pans and cool.

Shortcrust Pastry:

1 ⅓ cups flour
½ cup shortening
1 teaspoon salt
4 tablespoons cold water

Mix flour, shortening and salt and chop with a knife until consistency of breadcrumbs. Add water and stir with a fork until mixture forms a stiff dough. Keep as cool as possible. Roll out on wax paper and turn onto steak and kidney pie dish. Trim with leaf design. Brush with beaten egg and bake 375° F for 45 minutes.

This can be cooked ahead and reheated when needed. The cooked pie filling can be frozen, then defrosted and covered with pastry when needed. I find the pastry better if arranged on cold pie filling and put in 'fridge covered with plasic wrap uncooked. Then cook as above when required.

PAWPAW AU GRATIN

2 large green pawpaws
2 tablespoons butter
1 ¼ cups milk
2 - 3 ounces (⅓ cup) Cheddar cheese
2 teaspoons dry mustard
Parmesan cheese and breadcrumbs

Peel pawpaws, take out seeds and chop into smallish pieces. Cook in boiling salted water for 20 minutes until tender. Drain. Melt butter in a saucepan. Add flour, blend over low heat, add milk and heat to boiling until thickened, stirring constantly. Chop Cheddar cheese into small pieces and stir into sauce until dissolved. Season with salt, pepper and dry mustard. Mix with pawpaw. Turn into casserole dish, cover with breadcrumbs and grated Parmesan cheese. Place in low oven 300° F until ready to serve.

CHOCOLATE/ORANGE MOUSSE

6 ounces semi-sweet chocolate
2 ½ ounces (5 tablespoons) water
3 eggs
2 egg yolks
2 ½ ounces (⅓ cup) castor sugar
1 tablespoon (¼ ounce) gelatin
Juice 1 orange
2 ½ ounces (5 tablespoons) cream

Melt chocolate in water to form thick cream. Whisk the eggs, egg yolks and sugar together in basin over hot water until thick. Remove from heat and continue to whisk until bowl is cool. Add chocolate. Dissolve the gelatin in orange juice over heat, and add to mousse. Cool until thickening then fold in partially whipped cream. Turn into glass bowl and allow to set. Decorate with chopped nuts, more whipped cream and grated orange rind.

Mrs Anthony Gaade

Union Jack Dinner
for Six

Sausage and Bacon Pie*
Spinach and Endive Salad
Strawberry Mousse*

SAUSAGE AND BACON PIE

4 ounces (½ cup) lard
¼ pint (½ cup) water
12 ounces (3 cups) plain flour
Seasonings
2 onions, sliced
6 slices bacon
½ pound sausages
1 ounce (2 tablespoons) butter
4 tablespoons stuffing
1 egg beaten

Heat fat and water to melt fat. Gradually beat in flour and pinch of salt to form a thick dough. Knead on a floured board until smooth. Roll out ⅔ quite thinly and line a fluted pie mould or deep tin.

Fry onions, chopped bacon and sausages in butter until browned. Cut sausages into 1-inch pieces, add stuffing, season mixture and fill mould. Roll out rest of pastry to cover, seal edges and flute. Bake at 350° F for 1-1½ hours. For last 15 minutes remove from mould, brush pastry surface with beaten egg and increase heat to 400° F to brown crust. Allow to cool, then chill.

Adapt the filling to suit whatever leftovers you have - fish, eggs, vegetables, cold meats.

STRAWBERRY MOUSSE

1 pound canned strawberries
(drained reserving ½ cup juice)
½ cup water
1 package strawberry gelatin
1 cup double cream
2 egg whites

Reserve four whole strawberries for decoration. Chop remaining strawberries. Put juice and water into a saucepan. Bring to boil. Remove from heat. Add jelly and stir until dissolved. All to become cold. Whip the cream until thick. Remove about a quarter of the cream and reserve for decoration. Fold gelatin mixture into whipped cream. Stir in the chopped strawberries. Pour mixture into bowl. Let set in refrigerator. Decorate with strawberries and whipped cream.

Annette Herrington

Mrs David Herrington

❋❋❋❋❋❋❋❋❋

To prevent sea-sickness: mix 4 drachms bromide of soda, 2 drachms bromide of ammonia, and 3 ounces peppermint water. Take a teaspoonful in a wineglass of cold water before each meal and at bedtime for three days before the journey begins.

Lemon grass tea helps a cold.

Picnic and Barbecue

Barbecue at Government House

(for 6)

Salmon Mould Piquante*
Barbecued Chicken*
New Potatoes
Choice of vegetables
Orange Dessert*

SALMON MOULD PIQUANTE

1 tablespoon gelatin
¼ cup cold water
1½ teaspoons salt
1½ teaspoons prepared mustard
Dash cayenne
2 egg yolks, slightly beaten
¾ cup milk
1½ tablespoons melted butter
4 tablespoons lemon juice
1 cup flaked salmon
Lettuce

Soften gelatin in cold water 5 minutes. Combine seasonings, egg yolks and milk in top of double boiler, and cook over hot water 6 to 8 minutes or until thickened, stirring constantly. Add butter, lemon juice and gelatin, stirring until gelatin is dissolved. Remove from heat and fold in salmon. Turn into fish mould; chill until firm. Unmould on bed of crisp lettuce and serve.

BARBECUED CHICKEN

This is a good way of roasting chicken which has been deep frozen, and is rather lacking in flavour.

1 roasting chicken
1 teaspoon dry mustard
1 teaspoon ginger (optional)

1 teaspoon salt
Ground black pepper

Barbecue Sauce for Basting:

2 ounces (4 tablespoons) butter, melted
1 onion
1 tablespoon Worcestershire sauce
H.P. sauce
Tomato sauce (15 ounces)
Tomato pureé (6 ounces)
1 clove garlic

Chop onion finely and sauté in the butter, then add garlic, and all the liquids, and cook for half an hour and strain. Put the chicken in a roasting pan, mix the dry mustard, ginger, salt and ground pepper together and rub well into the chicken, place the roasting pan in a hot oven (350° F) and cook for twenty minutes. Now pour over the basting sauce and baste every quarter of an hour until cooked. Carve the chicken, skin fat from sauce, reduce a little and pour over the carved chicken.

ORANGE DESSERT

6 bitter Seville Oranges cut in quarters.

Soak oranges in cold water for 24 hours.

Cook very slowly in sugar syrup for several hours until tender. If necessary reduce the syrup to a marmalade consistency. Serve the quartered oranges in the syrup, cold. Serve with Petit Suisses or cream cheese.

Tangerines may be substituted if desired.

Lady Leather

❊ ❊ ❊ ❊ ❊ ❊ ❊ ❊ ❊

To cure headache, crush "Match-Me-If-You-Can" leaves and place on forehead and back of neck.

❊ ❊ ❊ ❊ ❊ ❊ ❊ ❊ ❊

Dinner Aboard Your Yacht!

(serves 4)

Quickest Ever Cold Soup*
Pepper Steaks*
Petits pois (or broccoli in season)
Romaine, Watercress and Chicory Salad
English Sherry Trifle*

QUICKEST EVER COLD SOUP

1⅓ large bars Philadelphia Cream Cheese (approximately 11 ounces)
1 can (10 ounces) consommé
Curry powder
Salt
Pepper

Put all in blender and chill several hours. This is then ready to serve.

PEPPER STEAKS

4 beef fillet steaks
Freshly ground black pepper
Seasoning pepper
Butter (for cooking)
4 teaspoons Cognac
stock
chopped parsley

Pound lots of freshly ground black pepper and seasoning pepper into steaks. The secret is to keep on pounding plenty of the pepper into the steaks. Sauté the steaks in hot butter in skillet for 3 to 4 minutes or so on each side. Flame with Cognac, then transfer to a warm oven while checking sauce. A little stock and butter may be added if necessary - then pour over the steaks. Garnish with parsley. Serve immediately.

ENGLISH SHERRY TRIFLE

Sliced jelly roll
dry sherry
Fruit of your choice
(Mandarin oranges are good, also strawberries!)
Bananas
Almonds
Custard
Whipped cream
Nuts for decoration

153

Line bottom of fruit bowl with sliced jelly roll. Soak with medium dry sherry and juice of the fruit you wish to use. Cover with the fruit and sliced bananas and almonds. Alternate these layers about 3 times with the jelly roll. Cover with "Birds" Custard (or boiled custard) and fresh whipped cream.

Easy! Takes 10 minutes!

Gill Reiss

Mrs Fred Reiss

Lamb Dinner for Six

Paradise Soup*
Grilled Butterfly Lamb*
Green beans and Almonds
Bermuda Potatoes*
Lemon Custard Fluff*

PARADISE SOUP
Easy and delicious - serves 6 - 8

5 cups tomato juice
1 cup sour cream
¼ cup grated onions
2 tablespoons lemon juice
1 teaspoon lemon rind
Salt and pepper to taste
¾ cup diced ham
Cucumber diced and seeded for garnish

Whisk tomato juice and sour cream together with all ingredients except ham and cucumber. Stir in ham and chill 4 hours. Sprinkle diced cucumber with basil and garnish soup just before serving.

GRILLED BUTTERFLY LAMB

Leg of lamb to serve six.
  Have butcher remove bone from leg of lamb. Marinate in your favourite marinade or use white wine, melted mint jelly and garlic clove. Charcoal as you would steak. Baste occasionally with marinade.

BERMUDA POTATOES

Scrub new potatoes. Melt ¼ pound butter in oven casserole with tight fitting lid. Add potatoes, cover and bake at 400° F. for about 20 minutes.

LEMON CUSTARD FLUFF
12 servings

4 eggs
1 cup sugar
3 tablespoons lemon juice
3 tablespoons lemon rind
½ cup water
1 package lemon Jello
1 cup cream, whipped
2 cups vanilla wafers, or graham crumbs

Mix yolks, ½ cup sugar, lemon juice and rind in top of double boiler. Cook until thick and smooth. Cool. Dissolve Jello in boiling water. Cool. Beat egg whites, adding remaining sugar gradually. Whip cream. Combine Jello and yolk mixture and fold in beaten whites and cream. Sprinkle ½ the crumbs in 9 x 13 pan, pour in lemon mixture and sprinkle remaining crumbs on top. Chill. I put a few strawberries on top if they are in season when serving.

Betty Hutchings

Mrs Ford Hutchings

Harbourfront Cook Out

Wahoo Steak*
Baked Potatoes
Corn-on-the-cob
Cantaloupe with Rum*

WILLIE FRITH'S WAHOO STEAK

Marinate wahoo steaks (1 or 1½ inches thick) in white wine for two hours.

Basting sauce:
Combine mayonnaise, lemon juice, Worcestershire sauce, hot pepper sauce, paprika and salt and pepper.

Spread this sauce over the wahoo steaks and grill them over a charcoal fire about ten minutes to a side, basting occasionally. Serve with lemon wedges and chopped parsley.

CANTALOUPE WITH RUM

½ cantaloupe per person
1 large honeydew melon
1 orange, sectioned
1 bunch seedless grapes
other berries or fruits in season
Fresh mint leaves
1 cup light rum
½ cup sugar
½ cup orange juice
2 tablespoons lemon juice

Cut the cantaloupe into halves; scoop out the seeds and stringy portion. Cut into balls or cubes, keeping shells intact. Make balls from honeydew. Combine rum, sugar, orange juice and lemon juice. Pour over the melon balls and other fruit. Chill. Just before serving fill the reserved cantaloupe shells with the fruit mixture. Garnish with fresh mint leaves.

Margaret de Marcy

Mrs Hubert de Marcy

Summer Barbecue

Barbecued Steaks
PawPaw and Cheese Casserole*
Garden Tomato Salad
Apricot Mousse

PAW PAW AND CHEESE CASSEROLE

Pick 3 medium-large green pawpaws. Cut in half, peel and seed. Slice the pawpaws about ¼" thick and cook in salted water until tender - approximately 14 minutes. Grease a 1½ quart casserole dish with butter. Arrange sliced pawpaws in dish and pour cheese sauce over same. Coat top with ½ cup grated cheese.

Bake at 400°F until brown. Serves 8.

CHEESE SAUCE

4 tablespoons butter or margarine
3 tablespoons flour
1 teaspoon salt
¼ teaspoon pepper
1½ cups milk
¾ cup grated cheese

Melt butter in saucepan. Add flour, salt and pepper and stir with wooden spoon. Set flame to medium-low, and slowly add milk while stirring constantly. Continue stirring over medium flame until mixture becomes thick. Add ¾ cup grated cheese. Continue stirring until cheese has melted.

Marilynn Simmons

Mrs R.D. Simmons

Mountain Trout Dinner
for Six

Quick Greek Lemon Soup*
Grilled Trout*
Buttered Carrots
Rosé de Provence
Watercress Salad
Spiced Pears*

QUICK GREEK LEMON SOUP

2 tins (10 ½ ounces each) chicken and rice soup
2 eggs, separated
juice of 2 lemons
grated rind of 1 lemon

Pour soup into large saucepan. Stir with whisk to separate rice. Bring to boil. Combine egg yolks with lemon juice and rind. Gradually stir a little of the hot soup into the yolk mixture and then pour it slowly back into the soup, stirring constantly. Beat the egg whites until they hold definite peaks and fold them into the hot soup. Let stand about three minutes before serving. (Serves 4-6)

GRILLED FRESH OR FROZEN TROUT

6 cleaned trout (12-14 ounces each)
salt
freshly ground pepper
1 tablespoon vegetable oil
1 cup heavy cream

Salt and pepper each trout inside and out, then rub the skin with oil. Place on a charcoal grill over a very hot fire and grill 3-4 minutes on each side. Lift the trout to a shallow pan just large enough to hold them and pour the cream over all the fish. Place the pan on the fire and bring to a boil. Cover and boil over high heat for exactly 2 minutes.
  Serve at once.

The grill must be immaculate, otherwise the skin of the trout will stick to it.

SPICED PEARS

2 tablespoons butter, melted
⅓ cup packed light brown sugar
½ teaspoon cinnamon
¼ teaspoon ginger
1 can (29 ounces) pear halves, drained
1 pint vanilla ice cream

Simmer all ingredients but the ice cream 10 minutes, turning pears once. Spoon ice cream in dessert glasses. Top with hot pears and their liquid. Serve immediately as hot pears melt the ice cream.

Mrs Allen Markelson

❄❄❄❄❄❄❄❄❄

Aloe juice helps sun burn and insect bites. It is also effective in drawing out thorns, cactus prickles and sea egg spines.

❄❄❄❄❄❄❄❄❄

Queen's Birthday Picnic
on the beach, boat, or Front Street

New Jersey Sloppy Joe's*
Cole Slaw - Potato Chips
Fruit Punch
(with rum for adults, without for children)
Cookie Cheesecake Squares*

NEW JERSEY SLOPPY JOE'S
(triple-decker sandwiches)

for each sandwich:
3 slices rye bread
1 slice ham, or tongue
1 slice turkey (optional)
1 slice Swiss cheese
2 tablespoons cole slaw
2 tablespoons Russian dressing
sweet butter

Spread each slice of rye bread with sweet butter and then with Russian dressing. On first slice of bread, place one slice of ham, one slice turkey, one slice Swiss cheese. Spread a bit of Russian dressing on this and place second slice of bread on top. Spread with cole slaw and then top with third piece of bread. Insert toothpicks through sandwich and slice in quarters. Wrap tightly in waxed paper.

Each sandwich serves one adult amply or two children. I make the cole slaw with Russian dressing and pineapple bits. To make RUSSIAN DRESSING: add equal parts mayonnaise and catsup and add salt and pepper and just enough vinegar to give it zip but not enough to make it runny.

COOKIE CHEESECAKE SQUARES
(24 bars)

1 roll plain refrigerator cookies, unbaked
¾ cup strawberry or any flavor preserves
1 8-ounce package cream cheese
1 cup dairy sour cream
1 egg
½ teaspoon vanilla

Slice cookie roll into ¼ inch slices; place slices in bottom of ungreased 13 x 9 inch disposable aluminium pan. Bake at 375° F for 12 to 15 minutes or until golden brown. Cookie dough will appear puffy when removed from oven. Gently spread with preserves.

In large mixer bowl, combine remaining ingredients and beat at medium speed until smooth. Pour this over the preserves, spreading to edges. Bake at 375° F for 25 to 30 minutes or until knife inserted in center comes out clean. Cool and take on picnic in pan. (Store in cooler). When ready to serve cut into bars.

Maria Smith

Mrs Edward Smith

Boat Menu

(serves 4-6)

Mushrooms on Toast*
Beef Curry and Rice*
Fruit Salad*
Fruit Scoop Cake*

If going on short weekend trips, I usually cook one large dish such as spaghetti sauce or a rich stew which I freeze and take frozen onto the boat. It defrosts during the day and is ready to be heated for supper. For the following night here is a suggested menu for mostly tinned items.

MUSHROOMS ON TOAST

Large can of mushrooms
1 lemon
1 tablespoon flour
1 glass of white wine or vermouth
pepper
Toast

Cook large can of mushrooms in their own juice in a frying pan until evaporates and they brown slightly. Add the juice of 1 lemon, sprinkle on flour and add white wine or vermouth, and a little pepper. Stir well and allow to thicken. Serve on toast.

BEEF CURRY

2 large onions, chopped
3 tablespoons oil

5 cloves
1 stick cinnamon
cardamom seeds
3 tablespoons curry powder
1 teaspoon cumin powder
1 teaspoon ginger
1 tin Walls stewing beef
1 tin tomato juice
1 small tin mixed vegetables
1 small tin potatoes (optional)
Chutney

Brown onions in oil. Add cloves, cinnamom and a few cardamom seeds and cook till onions are soft. Add curry powder, cumin powder and ginger. I combine all these at home in a small jar to take with me. Add 1 tin Walls stewing beef, cut up and mix well. Pour in tomato juice and mixed vegetables. Season with salt and simmer half an hour. Add potatoes (optional). Serve over hot rice with chutney.

If you cook extra rice, you can make a good rice salad for next day's lunch using cut up tomatoes, chopped green pepper, sliced hard boiled eggs, and a tin of tuna fish or crab. Season well and add mayonnaise to bind together.

FRUIT SALAD

Mix one orange and one grapefruit cut into sections with one can fruits for salad. Serve with tinned cream.

Mrs. William Meyer's
FRUIT SCOOP CAKE

1 cup sugar
1 cup flour
½ teaspoon salt
½ teaspoon cinnamon
½ teaspoon baking powder
½ teaspoon baking soda
1 egg, well beaten
1 teaspoon vanilla
¼ cup melted butter or margarine.
2 cups fruit
½ cup chopped nuts

Mix together flour, sugar, salt, cinnamon, baking powder and baking soda. Add egg, vanilla, and butter or margarine. Stir until moist. Mix in fruit and nuts. (Batter will be very thick). Turn into greased 8"x 8"x 2" pan and bake at 370° F for 30 minutes.

Any fruit can be used, chopped apples, drained canned fruit or dried fruit which should be soaked for ½ hour, drained and then chopped.

This cake is easy to make, travels well and is not too messy to eat on a boat.

Mrs Coles Diel

Picnic Lunch in the Boat
For Six

Len's Swizzles*
Scotch Eggs*
Macaroni Salad*
Brownies

LEN'S SWIZZLES

In a gallon thermos jug combine:

1 large can pineapple grapefruit juice (well chilled)
1 small can orange juice concentrate
1 small can Hawaiian punch concentrate
Juice of one large lemon (approximately 6 tablespoons)
20 ounces (approximately) Cockspur rum
10 ounces (approximately) Gosling's Black Seal rum

Add rum slowly and add to taste.
Be sure to leave some for your guests.
Fill the jug to the top with ice and swizzle!

SCOTCH EGGS

6 hard-cooked eggs
1 pound pork sausages
2 cups soft bread crumbs
1 teaspoon salt
½ teaspoon pepper
1 teaspoon thyme
1 teaspoon dry mustard
½ cup fine bread crumbs

Peel, rinse and dry the hard-cooked eggs. Remove meat from sausages by slitting up the side with a knife and removing skin. Mix together the sausage meat, soft bread crumbs, salt, pepper, thyme and dry mustard. It is best to do this with wet hands. Roll the mixture between two pieces of floured wax paper to one third inch thickness and cut into six portions. Wrap each egg with sausage meat and coat with the dry bread crumbs. Brown wrapped eggs on all sides in a quarter of an inch of oil. This will take about twenty minutes. Drain on paper towels. Can be served hot or cold.

When serving cut in half.

MACARONI SALAD

Yellow food colouring
8 ounces elbow macaroni
6 hard-cooked eggs
¾ cup diced green pepper
¼ cup diced pimento
½ cup diced sharp Cheddar cheese
2 teaspoons prepared mustard
2 teaspoons salt
½ cup finely chopped onions
Mayonnaise to moisten

Add food colouring to boiling salted water, enough to make the elbow macaroni a deep yellow. Cook macaroni according to package, rinse in cold water and drain. Chop the hard-cooked eggs and combine with the drained macaroni and remaining ingredients. Put in plastic serving container with cover and chill thoroughly. Garnish of parsley sprigs is pretty. Serves 6.

To serve this picnic, I cut the eggs in half and arrange them on one large plate. Everyone helps themselves. I serve the salad in paper bowls with a plastic fork. If you prefer, serve eggs and salad on one plate. If you don't care for swizzles, beer is excellent with this picnic.

Sally Gibbons

Mrs Leonard Gibbons

Lunch à la "Dividend"

(a boat picnic for 6-8)

Vichyssoise*
Deviled Eggs
Fresh Tuna Salad*
Macaroni Salad
Chilled white wine
Banana Bread

VICHYSSOISE

2-3 medium potatoes peeled and boiled with an onion
1 tin of cream of chicken soup
1 tin of evaporated milk
Place all ingredients in a blender. Blend until smooth.

This is the best recipe for vichyssoise that I have ever tried as it is so thick and rich.

FRESH TUNA SALAD, DADDY'S BEST

1 Daddy that catches fresh tuna
1 side of a small Blackfin tuna
Bay leaves
thyme
Juice of 6 lemons or limes

Place all the ingredients in a pot of water to cover the fish. Bring the water to a boil, and turn off!

Leave the fish in the water until it has completely cooled. Then flake up the meat and add chopped onion and celery. Add mayonnaise to taste.

This cooking method will remove the strong taste of the fish and everyone will love it.

Hope S. Berg

Mrs John Berg

For chest colds, fry onions in lard until brown, spread on gauze and apply hot to chest and back.

Picnic Lunch For 6

Gazpacho*
Pork Pie*
Green Salad
Fresh Fruit and/or cheeses

GAZPACHO

2 large tomatoes, peeled (1¾ pounds)
1 large cucumber, pared and halved
1 medium onion, peeled and halved
1 medium green pepper, seeded and halved
1 pimento, drained
2 cans tomato juice (12ounce size)
⅓ cup olive oil
⅓ cup red wine vinegar
¼ teaspoon Tabasco,
1½ teaspoons salt
⅛ teaspoon coarsely ground black pepper
2 cloves garlic, split
½ cup croutons
¼ cup chopped chives

In blender, pureé, covered, at high speed for 30 seconds:
1 tomato
½ cucumber
½ onion
¼ green pepper
all pimento
½ cup tomato juice

Pour this mixture into a bowl and mix it with the rest of the tomato juice plus ¼ cup olive oil, vinegar, Tabasco, salt and pepper. Place in refrigerator for 2 hours until thoroughly chilled.

Meanwhile, rub inside of a small skillet with garlic and reserve the piece of garlic. Then add rest of oil to pan, heat, and sauté croutons in oil until brown. Set aside.

Chop remaining tomato, onion, cucumber and green pepper and serve in individual dishes as condiments.

Crush remaining garlic in a garlic press and add to soup just before serving, stirring well.

Sprinkle the soup with chopped chives and croutons.

VERSATILE PORK PIE
[my own concoction]

Serve it hot with vegetables at home, cold with salad for a picnic, hot or cold in bite-size cubes at cocktail parties.

Line a greased pie dish with a short pastry.

In mixing bowl combine pork sausage meat with chopped onion, some fresh thyme, salt and pepper.

Place the mixture in pastry.

Fry a few slices of bacon until crisp, crumble and sprinkle on top of sausage mixture.

With butter, flour, milk and grated cheese, make a thick cheese sauce and spoon onto top of pie. Sprinkle with a little paprika.

Bake at 425° F for about ½ hour.

Pat Maher

Elegant Picnic Supper on the Boat
(for 6)

Crackers and Cheese
Rock Cornish Game Hens*
Cold Curried Rice*
Green Salad with Grapefruit Sections*
Niersteiner
Pecan Pie*

ROCK CORNISH GAME HENS

6 (approximately 1 pound each) Rock Cornish game hens, thawed
6 ounces apricot preserves
3 tablespoons lemon juice

Preheat oven to 450° F. Wash hens and pat dry with paper towels. Sprinkle cavities with salt and pepper. Arrange hens in roasting pan and brush with melted butter. Roast uncovered 40 minutes, brushing often with more melted butter. In a sauce pan melt the apricot preserves and stir in lemon juice. Brush hens with this mixture. Roast hens about 20 minutes longer until nicely glazed. Legs will move easily when they are cooked. Put in a plastic container to carry on the boat. *This doubles nicely to serve 12. You only need one more package of rice and 6 more hens!*

COLD CURRIED RICE

2 packages (6 ounces each) Uncle Ben's curried rice
¼ cup chopped drained chutney

Prepare rice as directed on the package. Stir in chutney. Put in covered plastic serving container and refrigerate for several hours.

GREEN SALAD WITH GRAPEFRUIT SECTIONS

1 head compact lettuce
2 grapefruits sectioned or 1 large tin grapefruit sections
Garlic French dressing, commercial

Take crisp lettuce in a plastic bag or in a container that will serve as a salad bowl. (I prefer to take a wooden salad bowl). Add drained grapefruit sections to greens when ready to serve and toss lightly with Garlic French Dressing. Serve in separate bowls. I use sections from two grapefruits well drained or 1 can of sections well drained. Sprinkle sections with a tablespoon of sugar first.

We think this is great on the boat because you can really enjoy the hens - pull them apart with your fingers and don't waste a single morsel. Just wash your hands overboard frequently! Also we think this is so special that we always take crystal wine glasses wrapped carefully in linen napkins - and always an extra bottle of wine!

PECAN PIE

1 unbaked pie shell (frozen ones are too small)

3 eggs
½ cup heavy cream less one tablespoon
1 cup sugar
1 teaspoon vanilla
2 tablespoons butter
1 tablespoon sherry
½ cup dark corn syrup
⅛ teaspoon salt
1 ½ cups pecans, and enough to decorate

Put everything in this order in the blender and blend for 10 seconds. Put mixture into pie shell and bake at 400° F for 25 minutes. Put on the decorative pecans and bake 10 minutes more. Cool before serving.

If you serve this in small wedges with small clusters of icy cold green grapes it will serve 12. It is very rich but I've never brought any home! This is also quite nice made with walnuts.

Sally Gibbons

Mrs Leonard Gibbons

Buffet and Cocktails

Buffet Frio
(cold Chilean buffet for 16 to 20)

Torta de Panqueques (seafood and crêpe cake)*
Huevos à la Huancaina (eggs and peanuts)*
Pollos Escabechados (chicken or game birds in aspic)*
Tajadas Delgadas de Roast Beef (platter of sliced cold beef)
Ensalada de Tomates (tomato salad)
Ensaladas Verdes (green salad)
red and chilled white wines
Crema de Cafe (coffee cream)*

TORTA DE PANQUEQUES

24 very thin 10-inch crêpes (unsweetened)
2 7 ½-ounce cans crabmeat (or lobster, fish or chicken)
2 9-ounce packages French-cut frozen green beans
6 tomatoes
2 10-ounce packages frozen corn niblets
2 cups homemade mayonnaise (approximately)
4 avocados
Lemon juice

This is a meal in itself and the variations are unlimited. It consists of thin pancakes with various fillings sandwiched between them. The assembled pancakes are covered with mashed avocado and served cold.

Combine drained crabmeat with enough mayonnaise to hold it together. Sprinkle with lemon juice. Mix cooked and chilled beans with salad oil and season to taste. Combine cooked and cooled corn niblets and mayonnaise. Season the peeled and thinly sliced tomatoes and toss with oil.

Place a crêpe on serving platter, spread with crab. Cover with a second crêpe, spread with mayonnaise, then beans. Crêpe, mayonnaise, tomatoes. Crêpe, corn and mayonnaise. Continue alternating fillings and crêpes until 12 crêpes have been used. (Start and finish with a crêpe). This makes one cake, serving 8 to 10 people. Use the remaining crêpes and fillings to make another cake. Crêpes and fillings may be made in advance but should be assembled only 4 or 5 hours before serving. Chill.

Cut and peel avocados, cover with cold water and lemon juice for about ½ hour. Drain and mash with more lemon juice, salt and pepper and 1 teaspoon milk. Cover crêpe cakes completely with avocado mixture just before serving. Decorate with sliced ripe olives.

HUEVOS A LA HUANCAINA

12 eggs (hard-boiled)
2 medium onions (finely chopped or grated)
1 cup mayonnaise (homemade)
2 cups cream-style cottage cheese
2 cups freshly toasted ground peanuts
mustard
Tabasco or Red Devil sauce
salt and pepper

Combine mayonnaise, onions, cottage cheese and 1 cup peanuts. Add salt, pepper, mustard and Tabasco to taste. (It must be quite hot). Cut the cold eggs in half crosswise (not lengthwise) and arrange on platter, yolk side down. Pour mayonnaise mixture over them and sprinkle with remaining peanuts. Decorate with bib-style lettuce.

POLLOS ESCABECHADOS

4 pounds chicken thighs (defrosted)
2 pounds chicken drumsticks (defrosted)
10 medium onions cut in fourths
10 carrots cut in round slices
2 crushed cloves of garlic (or garlic salt)
6 cups salad oil
3 cups white vinegar

2 tablespoons black peppercorns
salt
Fresh parsley

Place chicken parts in one large (or two small sauce pans) with the onions, carrots, garlic, salt and peppercorns. Add oil and vinegar. Cover and boil briskly for three minutes. Lower heat and simmer until chicken is tender. (About 30 to 45 minutes). Shake sauce pan occasionally to prevent sticking. Leave in sauce pan until cool. Arrange chicken pieces on serving platter with carrots and onions on top of them and around edge. Pour sauce overall to about one-inch depth. Refrigerate until serving time. (Sauce turns to jelly in about 6 hours). Decorate with parsley.

CREMA DE CAFE

2 6-ounce cans Nestle's cream or heavy cream
8 tablespoons of sugar
6 teaspoons of arrowroot or cornstarch
4 teaspoons of instant coffee
4 eggs

Mix the cream with the sugar and arrowroot and cook very slowly for 3 minutes, stirring constantly with wooden spoon. Cool slightly and add the instant coffee and beaten egg yolks. Beat egg whites until stiff but not dry. Fold into coffee mixture. Pour into champagne glasses and chill. Top with whipped cream and ground walnuts. May be made the night before. This is for 12 servings, double recipe for 24.

Veronica Naylor

Mrs Charles Naylor

Christmas Cocktails

Mulled Wine and Mincemeat Pies*
(Old English Tradition)

MULLED WINE

The simplest mulled wine is made by dissolving sugar in a little water; about 4 ounces (½ cup) of sugar to ¼ pint (½ cup) water for each bottle of red wine. Bring the water and sugar to a boil. Toss a couple of cloves into the pot, add the wine and bring up to boiling point, but no more - stir occasionally with a cinnamon stick. Remove from stove. Grate a little nutmeg over the top and serve very hot.

This recipe can be prepared easily and swiftly to meet demand as the party progresses! Keep warm in a big tureen on a hotplate.

MINCE PIES
Makes two dozen individual pies

Pastry:
10 ounces (2 ½ cups) flour
1 ounce (3 tablespoons) ground almonds
6 ounces (¾ cup) butter or 1 ½ sticks
3 ounces (½ cup) sugar
Rind of ½ lemon
1 egg yolk
3 tablespoons milk

Filling:
1 pound mincemeat
1 - 2 tablespoons brandy

Sift the flour into a mixing bowl and add the ground almonds. Add the butter, cut in small pieces and rub into the mixture evenly. Add the sugar and grated lemon rind. Lightly mix the egg yolk and milk and stir into the dry ingredients. Mix to a fairly firm dough, turn out onto a lightly floured board and knead until smooth. Chill for 30 minutes before using.

Roll the pastry out onto a lightly floured working surface and, using a plain or fluted cutter, stamp out 48 circles of the pastry.

Place 24 in lightly greased tartlet tins - prepare in batches if necessary. Mix the mincemeat with the brandy and place a teaspoonful of the mixture in the centre of each pastry circle. Take care not to overfill the pies. Dampen the edges of the pastry and cover each one with a pastry top. Seal the edges and then, using scissors, snip two slits in the top of each. Place in the centre of a hot oven (400° F) and bake for 15 - 20 minutes or until golden brown.

Dust with icing sugar and serve hot.

These pies can be made in advance and reheated or they can be frozen in their tins before cooking.

Mrs I.A.C. Kinnear

Holiday Buffet Dinner
(Serves Eight)

Caesar Salad*
Baked Lasagna Verde*
Garlic Bread
Pears Sabayon*

CAESAR SALAD

Romaine and Iceberg lettuce, cut up
1 teaspoon strong mustard
3 cloves garlic, crushed
1 teaspoon salt
drop of Worcestershire sauce
pinch of oregano
4 tablespoons wine vinegar
4-5 tablespoons salad oil
1-2 tablespoons chopped fresh parsley
8 anchovies, cut up
juice of 1-2 fresh lemons
½ cup grated Parmesan cheese
  or
¼ cup grated Parmesan cheese and
¼ cup grated Swiss cheese
2 eggs, boiled 1-1½ minutes
freshly ground pepper
garlic bread croutons

Mix mustard, garlic and salt together. Add a good drop of Worcestershire sauce and a pinch of oregano. Mix well with vinegar and oil. Add parsley and anchovies to dressing. Then add lemon juice and grated cheese.

Put lettuce in a large pot (Dutch oven), pour over dressing and crack eggs over it. Add ground pepper and croutons. Mix well to coat evenly. Serve on individual salad plates.

LASAGNA VERDE

12 lasagna green spinach noodles

Meat Sauce:
2 large onions, finely chopped
2 large cans (15 ounces each) tomato sauce
1 can (6 ounces) tomato paste
2 pounds ground sirloin
3 cloves garlic, finely chopped

salt and pepper
1 can (15 ounces) tomato juice.
1 teaspoon paprika

White Sauce:
3 tablespoons butter
3 tablespoons flour
3 cups warm milk
salt and pepper
pinch dry mustard
handful grated Parmesan cheese

3 packages frozen chopped spinach - cooked as directed and drained.
2 pounds Ricotta cheese
Grated Swiss and Parmesan cheeses

Noodles: Fill a large pot nearly to the top with salted water. Add ½ glass oil and bring to a boil. Cook lasagna noodles one at a time to avoid them sticking together. Remove them with spatulas and place them on paper towels to dry.

Meat Sauce: Sauté onions and garlic in ¼ cup salad oil until glazed over medium heat, add meat, stirring constantly until brown. Add tomato sauce and paste. Stir well. Add tomato juice, paprika, salt and pepper to taste. Simmer ½ hour.

White Sauce: In medium saucepan, slowly heat butter just until melted and golden, not browned. Remove from heat. Add flour and combine well. Add milk, a little at a time, stirring after each addition. Over medium heat, bring to boiling, stirring constantly. Reduce heat and simmer one minute. Then add salt and pepper to taste, pinch of dry mustard and grated cheese. Stir well over low heat, just until cheese is melted.

In a rectangular 9 x 13 inch pyrex dish, put one ladle of meat sauce to cover bottom. Place noodles on top. Sprinkle spinach over noodles. Crumble Ricotta cheese over spinach. Cover with meat sauce, then with white sauce. Sprinkle grated cheeses over sauce. Repeat procedure twice beginning again with lasagna noodles.

Bake in preheated 350° F oven for 30 - 35 minutes, or until cheese is melted and lasagna is heated through.

PEARS SABAYON

1 cup granulated sugar
4 fresh pears, pared, halved and cored
  or
  1 large can Bartlett pears halved

Sauce:
4 egg yolks
1 cup confectioners sugar
¼ cup sherry (Bristol Cream, if possible)
¾ cup heavy cream

In 4 quart saucepan, combine granulated sugar and 3 cups water, heat until sugar dissolves. Add pears, cover, simmer gently until tender - about 30 minutes. Remove from heat. Carefully place pears, with about 1 cup syrup, in bowl. Refrigerate several hours.

Sauce: In top of double boiler, with rotary beater or wire wisk, beat egg yolks, sugar, and sherry until light. Place over hot, not boiling, water; water should not touch bottom of double boiler top. Cook, stirring constantly, 8-10 minutes. Refrigerate several hours. Mixture thickens on standing.

In medium bowl beat cream until soft peaks form when beater is raised. Carefully fold in chilled sauce.

Drain pears. Serve topped with sauce.

Barbara Elkin

Mrs. J. J. Elkin

Dinner for A Cast of Thousands
(Actually I only fed 30!)

Various cheeses and crackers
Mary Jane Pantry's Clam Dip*
Lasagna*
Tossed Green Salad
Garlic Bread*
Fresh Fruit Compote*

MARY JANE PANTRY'S CLAM DIP

Mix together one tin (drained) minced clams with three large packages (8 ounces each) cream cheese seasoned with a couple of dollops of Worcestershire sauce. Beat with hand mixer (or your own arm if you want to develop some outstanding biceps) adding a little of the clam juice to make desired consistency.

LASAGNA

This recipe serves 24 people, and I doubled it for a party of 30, which gave me a couple of wonderful portions to freeze and have a couple of quick, easy meals from.

4 pounds hamburger
2 cups chopped onion
2 cloves minced garlic (I use a garlic press)
2 tins tomatoes (14 ½ ounces each), chopped
2 tins tomato sauce (15 ounces)
3 tablespoons parsley flakes
salt
2 cartons cottage cheese (2 pounds each)
1 cup grated Parmesan cheese
2 tablespoons parsley flakes again
2 tablespoons oregano
salt
16 ounces lasagna noodles
1 ½ pounds Mozzarella cheese
Parmesan

Brown hamburger, onion and garlic. Add chopped tomatoes, tomato sauce, parsley and salt. Cook slowly for about an hour. I thicken this mixture with corn starch just because I don't like it too watery (and it's even better if you make a paste with wine and corn starch). Mix cottage cheese, Parmesan cheese, parsley, oregano and salt. Cook the noodles according to the directions.

In one of the large disposable aluminium foil baking pans, put a layer of noodles, layer of hamburger sauce and a layer of Mozzarella, topped with a layer of the cottage cheese mixture. Repeat. Top the last layer of noodles with the sauce mixture and sprinkle generously with Parmesan cheese. Cook at 350° F for about 45 minutes.

GARLIC BREAD

I cut the loaf of French bread into slices about an inch thick, so the slice is severed all the way through. In a small frying pan I melt a good hunk of butter and press a couple of garlic buds into it. When butter is melted, I dip each slice on one side into the butter and garlic, and replace it in the loaf. Wrap loaf in aluminum foil and heat in oven.

FRESH FRUIT COMPOTE

This one's a labour of love, but a delightfully spectacular dessert.

I buy a watermelon and scoop out the inside with a melon baller, and when I couldn't get any more balls out, I scooped and smotted the melon. In a large mixing bowl, I put about ½ the watermelon balls without their liquid, and a box each, including their liquid, of frozen strawberries, frozen raspberries and frozen bing cherries, as well as a jar of orange and grapefruit slices with their liquid (actually ambrosia is better if it's available) and some chopped coconut. I then put this mixture back into the empty watermelon halves, adding more melon balls to each half as needed. You can add a bit of kirsch to this mixture if you wish. And for goodness sake, be careful carrying them - it's easy to spill!

Joan Skinner

Mrs David Skinner

Summer Buffet for Eight

Artichoke Hearts Vinaigrette
Bermuda Rockfish Robert*
Ala Pilaf*
Molded Gazpacho Salad*
French Loaf with Parmesan Butter
Brandy Alexander Pie*

BERMUDA ROCKFISH ROBERT

1 heaping cup almonds
1 egg
¾ cup milk
4 large fillets rockfish

Chop nuts finely in blender, spread on waxed paper. Blend egg and milk, dip fillets into mixture. Coat each side of fillets with ground nuts. Fry in 3 tablespoons foaming butter, seasoning with salt and white pepper on each side. Serve immediately.

ALA PILAF

2-3 teaspoons butter
1 ½ cups Bulghur Wheat
½ medium onion finely chopped
½ teaspoon oregano
1 teaspoon chopped parsley
2 chicken bouillon cubes
2 cups water
Salt and pepper

Sauté onions in large skillet till clear. Then add Bulghur wheat and brown lightly. Make a depression in center and pour in 2 cups boiling water with 2 bouillon cubes, mix well and add oregano, parsley, salt and pepper.

Cover and simmer on low heat until fluffy like rice.

This best in an electric skillet. When done it can be turned off and reheated in pan with ¼ cup of water added.

MOULDED GAZPACHO

3 envelopes gelatin
1 can (18 ounces) tomato juice
⅓ cup wine vinegar
1 teaspoon salt
Tabasco
2 medium tomatoes, chopped
1 large cucumber, chopped
1 medium green pepper (diced)
¼ cup finely chopped onion
1 clove garlic minced
1 teaspoon chopped chives
3 large ripe avocados (optional)

In a medium saucepan sprinkle gelatin over ¾ cup of the tomato juice. Heat gently, stirring until gelatin has dissolved. Remove from heat.

Stir in remaining tomato juice, wine vinegar, salt and a few drops of Tabasco. Cool until it is the texture of egg white. Fold in tomatoes, cucumber, pepper, onion, garlic, chives. Pour into oiled mould.

Avocados may be added, used as garnish or both. Delicious even without.

For dessert we often serve very rich Brandy Alexanders made in the blender with lots of heavy cream and sprinkled with nutmeg. Or, if we are ambitious:

BRANDY ALEXANDER PIE

1 envelope gelatin
½ cup cold water
⅔ cup sugar
3 eggs, separated
¼ cup Cognac
¼ cup Crème de Cacao
2 cups heavy cream, whipped
1 nine-inch graham cracker crust
Grated chocolate garnish

Sprinkle gelatin over cold water in a saucepan. Add ⅓ cup sugar, salt and egg yolks. Stir to blend. Heat gelatin mixture over low heat while stirring until gelatin dissolves and mixture thickens. Do not boil. Remove from heat and stir in Cognac and Crème de Cacao. Chill until mixture begins to mound slightly. Beat the egg whites until stiff. Gradually beat in remaining sugar and fold into thickened mixture. Fold in one cup of the whipped cream. Chill several hours before serving.

Garnish with remaining whipped cream and chocolate.

Jaue Odenweller

Mrs Robert Odenweller

❄

Festive Winter Buffet
(Serves 25 - 30)

Mushroom Tarts*
Assorted Nibblers
Cold Sliced Roast Turkey
Cold Sliced Roast Ham
Cranberry - Orange Relish*
Mustard - Pickles
Opa's Herring Salad*
Macaroni and Cheese Casserole
Green Salad with Choice of Dressing
Hot Yeast Rolls
Sweets Tray
Coffee

I usually prepare for such dinners at least one week in advance, I make and freeze the macaroni and cheese, rolls and sweets.

The mushroom tarts and nibblers such as olives, onion, pickles, cheese cubes, etc., are passed while the guests enjoy cocktails. The main meal is set out in the dining room just before the guests arrive, except for the macaroni and cheese and rolls, which I bring in at the last minute to a warming tray from the oven. The guests then help themselves to the buffet, find a comfortable place to sit and enjoy their meal. They can then help themselves to coffee, and the sweets tray is passed. I like to include petit fours, small frosted brownies, chocolate mints and sugared almonds.

MUSHROOM TARTS

75 frozen cocktail-size pastry shells
2 pounds fresh mushrooms, finely chopped
2 large garlic cloves, mashed

¾ cup butter
¼ cup dry sherry
½ tablespoon salt
⅛ teaspoon pepper
4 tablespoons parsley, chopped
4 tablespoons fresh or freeze dried chives
1 cup dairy sour cream

The day before party sauté mushrooms and garlic in butter three minutes in large skillet, add sherry, continue cooking until liquid has evaporated. Add next four ingredients. Remove from heat and add sour cream. Let cool and store in refrigerator covered.

Two hours before guests arrive, bake pastry shells and fill with 1 tablespoon mushroom mixture. When guests arrive these are warmed in oven (350° F for 8 minutes) and served.

CRANBERRY - ORANGE RELISH

1 pound fresh cranberries
2 oranges
1 pound sugar

Wash cranberries and sort. Put cranberries through food chopper. Peel, section and chop oranges. Add sugar and mix well.

OPA'S HERRING SALAD

This is my father's speciality. It is traditionally served in Germany on Christmas Eve but we love it year round.

1 small jar pickled beets and juice
1 small jar celery hearts
1 small can diced carrots
½ jar capers
1 small jar dill pickles
1 large jar Bismarck Herring and liquid
3 to 4 boiled potatoes, peeled
2 to 3 diced apples
3 diced hard-boiled eggs
1 large carton sour cream
salt and freshly ground pepper

Dice all ingredients as small as possible. Mix together and add liquid from herring. Season with salt and pepper. Fold in sour cream and store in refrigerator until chilled. To serve, heap in center of lettuce leaves on deep platter.

Maria Smith
Mrs Edward Smith

Buffet Party
(For 8)

Spinach Hors-d'oeuvre*
Sausage and Rice Casserole*
Herb Bread*
Green Salad
Ginger Mousse*

SPINACH HORS-D'OEUVRE

2 packages frozen chopped spinach
4 hard boiled eggs, chopped
1 medium onion, finely chopped
1-2 tablespoons Miracle Whip (only)
dash of Worcestershire Sauce
Salt and pepper

Cook and drain spinach. Allow to cool, then mix with eggs, onion, Worcestershire sauce, salt and pepper. Add Miracle Whip last and use only enough to mix ingredients thoroughly. Transfer to serving bowl, garnish with parsley and serve with crackers.

This cannot be frozen, but it can be made several hours in advance.

SAUSAGE AND RICE CASSEROLE

8 tablespoons butter
1 cup finely chopped onions
1 ½ cups rice (not the quick cooking kind)
3 ½ cups chicken broth
½ teaspoon white pepper
½ teaspoon saffron or the flower of one marigold
2 pounds sweet Italian sausage or beef sausage,
    cut in 1 inch pieces
1 pound mushrooms, sliced
½ pound cooked diced ham (optional)

Sauté onions in butter about 10 minutes or until transparent. Stir in rice until it is.coated with butter. Add broth, pepper and saffron or marigold and bring to boil. Cover and bake at 350° F for 10 minutes. Remove cover and bake 25 minutes or until liquid is absorbed. Meanwhile, brown sausages, mushrooms and ham. Drain and add to casserole when liquid is absorbed. Mix well, top with a sprinkling of Parmesan cheese and cook uncovered for another 5 minutes.

It has been my experience that rice does not freeze well, nor does it keep in the refrigerator. This casserole should be made the day of serving and reheated just before dinner.

HERB BREAD

Chopped parsley
Chives
Oregano
Dried Thyme and Dill

Mix ingredients with butter and spread between layers of French bread. Wrap in tin foil and bake 20 minutes at 350° F.

GINGER MOUSSE
(serves 10)

Residents from the lower parishes who have had the pleasure of dinner at Sheila Gosling's house, will recognize this taste treat. It is known by another name, but readers will have to approach Sheila for it. This is truly the best dessert I have ever eaten.
  This should be made the morning of the party and refrigerated.

1 quart heavy whipping cream
2 teaspoons chopped green ginger
1 small can shredded coconut
1 large tin chopped walnuts
½ cup sugar
9 tablespoons Drambuie
2 tablespoons Scotch
1 box of ginger snaps

Whip cream until stiff with sugar. Add next six ingredients one at a time, ending with Scotch. Mix well. Layer in a large serving bowl between ginger snaps until whipped cream mixture is exhausted. Make sure that the last layer is whipped cream, and remember to make thick layers.

Jane West

Mrs Stephen West

❀❀❀❀ ❀❀❀❀❀

Shark oil poured into a bottle and placed in a sunny spot makes a reliable barometer.

❀❀❀❀❀❀❀❀❀

Cocktail Crush for 50

Pizza*
Pâté Maison*
Cheese Straws*
. Cheese Ball*
Liverwurst Pâté*
Hot Seafood Hors-d'oeuvre*
Caviar on Toast*
Artichoke Hearts and Ham Bites*
Assorted Quiches
Fresh Vegetable Platter*
Cheese Fondue
Cheese Biscuits

PIZZA

This recipe makes one 12-14 inch diameter pizza:

Pastry:
2 ¼ cups flour
½ cup water
½ ounce yeast
2 tablespoons lard
pinch of salt

Topping:
¼ cup butter
2 tomatoes, sliced
2 onions, chopped
3 mushrooms
2 cups Cheddar cheese (or Parmesan)
red hot sauce
oregano
salami or pepperoni
1 green pepper, seeded and chopped
anchovies
2 cloves garlic, crushed
4-6 tablespoons tomato purée

Rub fat into flour and salt. Heat water to lukewarm and dissolve yeast in it. Make well in center of fat and flour mixture and add liquid to make dough. Knead and form into large disk. Lay this on baking sheet or pizza pan and let stand for 15 minutes.

In a skillet, melt butter and sauté onions and green pepper. Add garlic, mushrooms and tomatoes. Add tomato purée, oregano, hot sauce, and some of the grated cheese. Arrange salami slices and anchovies on dough. Spread the sauce over these, leaving most of the liquid behind. Raise the edges of the pizza so sauce won't overflow. Sprinkle with the remaining cheese. Bake immediately in 400° F oven for 15 minutes.

This can be made ahead and frozen. Also it can be made in the shape of oblong baking sheets, to be cut into bite size pieces.

PATE MAISON

1 pound livers (chicken, calves or pigs)
¼ pound lean pork, diced
¼ pound lard, diced
1 clove garlic, crushed
2 tablespoons chopped onion
½ pound streaky bacon
1 ounce (2 tablespoons) butter
salt, pepper, thyme, bay leaf, chervil, parsley
4 - 5 ounces brandy
2 ½ ounces fresh cream
1 egg

Cut away excess sinews from liver and cut into 1-inch dice. In skillet, melt butter and add liver, onions, garlic and herbs. Add lean pork and lard. Cook over medium heat for a few minutes. Then blend in blender, or mince twice. Line mould or 8x4x2 inch pyrex dish with bacon, allowing ends to drape over sides of dish. Add egg to minced pâté to bind together. Add brandy and cream and beat with wooden spoon. Turn into mould and fold over ends of bacon to cover top of pâté. Sit dish in a pan of hot water in a 350° F oven for 2 hours. Turn off oven and leave pâté to set in turned off oven all night. Cover pâté with lid or foil if it gets too brown on top.

Serve on biscuits or rusks.

CHEESE STRAWS

Puff pastry
Parmesan cheese
Cayenne pepper

Rinse a baking sheet with water and roll out puff pastry onto it - about ¼ -inch thick. Brush pastry with eggwash (egg yolk with a few drops of water added) and sprinkle liberally with Parmesan cheese and cayenne. Cut pastry into long thin strips. These strips can be twisted or made into circles. Bake at 400° F for approximately 10 minutes.

CHEESE BALL

Mix equal quantities of cream cheese, grated Cheddar cheese and blue cheese. Mould this mixture into a ball - flattened on the bottom to sit on a plate. Cover the cheese ball with chopped parsley. Serve with biscuits.

BRAUNSCHWEIGER LIVERWURST PATE

1 pound liverwurst
½ pound cream cheese
Cognac
Worcestershire sauce

Mix liverwurst with ¼ pound cream cheese and Cognac to taste. Mould into desired shape and chill. Make topping with remaining cheese softened with milk and Worcestershire sauce. Spread this over pâté and decorate with parsley and raw mushroom slices. Serve with biscuits.

HOT SEAFOOD HORS-D'OEUVRE

10 ounce can mussels, drained
10 ounce can clams, drained
10 ounce can oysters
16 ounces cream cheese
1 cup sour cream
½ cup sherry

Combine all ingredients and bake at 300° F for 20 - 30 minutes. Serve hot on biscuits or rusks.

CAVIAR ON TOAST

Mix black caviar with sour cream. Cut bread in bite size pieces and toast in oven. Spread with caviar mixture and reheat.

ARTICHOKE HEARTS AND HAM BITES

1 14-ounce can artichoke hearts
6 slices boiled ham
½ cup olive oil
2 lemons
salt, pepper

Drain artichoke hearts, cut in half. Make dressing with olive oil, lemon, salt and pepper to taste. Garlic powder may be added if desired. Marinate artichoke hearts in dressing overnight. Cut ham into 1x4 inch strips and wrap around artichoke hearts. Secure with toothpick. Bake at 300° F for 10 minutes.

FRESH VEGETABLE PLATTER

Cut any of the following into bite sized pieces:

Carrots
Celery
Cucumber
Broccoli
Cauliflower
Lettuce leaves (small whole ones)
Scallions
Tomatoes
Boiled potatoes
Green pepper
Endive (small whole leaves)
Artichoke leaves - cooked and trimmed

Serve these arranged attractively on a large plate with one of the following dips:

1. Equal quantities of mayonnaise and ketchup seasoned with English mustard, salt and pepper.
2. 1 cup mayonnaise
   3 ounces Neufchatel cheese, softened (or blue)
   1 teaspoon mixed herbs
   Worcestershire sauce, salt and pepper to taste
3. 3 ounces cream cheese, softened
   1 cup sour cream
   2 tablespoons chopped chives
   2 tablespoons chopped parsley
   1 tablespoons anchovy paste
   2 teaspoons lemon juice
   dash freshly ground pepper
4. Crab dip:
   8 ounces cream cheese, softened
   ¼ cup mayonnaise
   ¼ cup cocktail sauce
   2 teaspoons mustard
   7 ounce tin flaked crabmeat
   ⅓ cup finely chopped celery
   2 tablespoons finely chopped parsley

Mary Walker

Mrs B.W. Walker

January Buffet Special
(for Six)

Shrimp on Ice in Lettuce-lined Bowl
Cocktail Sauce
Beef Stroganoff*
Noodles
Salad Vinaigrette
Mocha Chocolate Bavarian*

BEEF STROGANOFF

2 pounds sirloin, cut in ¾ -inch cubes
Flour
4 tablespoons fat
1 cup chopped onion
2 cloves garlic, minced
2 cups mushrooms, drained
2 cups sour cream
1 10-ounce can condensed tomato soup
1 6-ounce can tomato paste
2 tablespoons Worcestershire sauce
8 drops Tabasco sauce
1 teaspoon salt
Dash pepper
2 8-ounce packages noodles, cooked
Parmesan cheese

Dip meat in flour; brown in hot fat. Add onion, garlic and mushrooms.
   Combine sour cream, tomato soup, tomato paste, mushroom liquid and seasonings; pour over meat. Simmer till tender, about 1 hour.
   Serve over hot noodles. Sprinkle with Parmesan cheese.

BLENDER MOCHA CHOCOLATE BAVARIAN

¼ cup cold water
2 envelopes unflavoured gelatin
2 teaspoons instant coffee
½ cup boiling water
1 cup semi-sweet chocolate chips
1 tablespoon sugar
⅛ teaspoon salt
½ teaspoon vanilla extract
2 egg yolks
1 cup heavy cream
1 ½ cups crushed ice, drained

Put cold water, **gelatin and instant** coffee into blender container, add boiling water, cover and process at STIR until gelatin is dissolved, (about one minute). Add chocolate, sugar, salt and vanilla. Continue processing until mixture is smooth. Add egg yolks, cream and crushed ice and continue processing until mixture begins to thicken. Pour at once into serving dishes.

Let set 5 to 10 minutes before serving.

Patti von Bieren

Mrs Karl von Bieren

❧

Small Cocktail Party

Quiche Lorraine
Hot Tuna Dip*
Cucumber Sandwiches*

HOT TUNA DIP

2 cans (7-ounces each) tuna fish
8 ounces cream cheese
mayonnaise
chives
curry powder
dash of sherry
chopped almonds

Drain tuna well and mix with softened cream cheese. Add mayonnaise to make a soft consistency. Add chives and curry to taste, and a dash of sherry. Sprinkle with chopped almonds. Bake in oven-proof serving dish at 350° F for 20 minutes. Serve hot on crackers.

CUCUMBER SANDWICHES

Marinate peeled and thinly sliced cucumbers in oil and vinegar for several hours. Drain.

Cut rounds from white bread. Spread mayonnaise on the bread and top with cucumber slice, salt and pepper. (The bread may be cut and the mayonnaise spread several hours ahead but add cucumbers just before serving).

Sally Cooper

Mrs Alex Cooper

Celebration at "Kiskadee"

(Serves 24 - 30)

Banquet Chicken Noodles*
Green Salad
Kiskadee Fantasy*
Demi-tasse

BANQUET CHICKEN NOODLES

8 - 10 pounds chicken
2 pounds mushrooms, sliced
1 green pepper, diced
1 cup butter
10 tablespoons flour
4 cups chicken broth
1 cup heavy cream
2 egg yolks, beaten
2 pimentos, sliced
salt to taste
3 6-ounce boxes broad noodles
1 cup seasoned bread crumbs

Simmer chicken in seasoned water until tender. Remove bones and cut into medium sized pieces. Cook mushrooms and pepper in ¾ cup of the butter until tender. Add and blend flour. Add broth (in which chicken was cooked), then cream, stirring constantly until smooth and thick. Pour slowly over egg yolks and blend. Add pimentos and salt. Place noodles (cooked to just underdone) in casseroles (total 6 quarts), add chicken, pour over mushroom-cream sauce. Top with bread crumbs mixed with remaining butter, melted. Bake 30 minutes in 300° F oven until golden on top.

KISKADEE FANTASY
(Serves 8, multiply recipe for required servings)

28 saltines crumbed with rolling pin
⅓ cup melted butter
Blend and press into pie pan.

3 egg whites beaten stiff adding 1 cup of sugar during beating, add 1 teaspoon white vinegar and 1 teaspoon vanilla. Put in pie shell and bake for 10 minutes until pale gold at 300° F. When cold add medium size tin of crushed well-drained pineapple (or other fruit). Top with 1 cup cream, whipped. Delicious! But do not substitute saltines.

Mrs Phyllis West Harron

INDEX

Index continued on next page

Cut Here · *Cut Here*

Bermuda Junior Service League

Post Office Box 1226
Hamilton 5
BERMUDA

Please send me . . . . . copies of Bermudian Cookery at $4.50 per copy surface mail or $5.00 per copy air mail (postage and handling included). (U.K. £2 surface mail or £2.20 air mail.) Enclosed is my check or money order for $. . . . .

Name . . . .

Address . . . .

City . . . .   Country . . . .

(Make checks payable to: Bermuda Junior Service League — Cookbook)